Beyond the Breakers

A SUBUD ODYSSEY

SILVANA WANIUK

WITH A FOREWORD BY
ANTHONY BRIGHT-PAUL

Subud is a spiritual process, not a theory or a teaching. Statements about Subud should be considered as reflecting the author's own personal experience and understanding. They are not to be regarded as authoritative pronouncements nor are they intended to be a Subud doctrine. For information about Subud, see the Glossary.

Front Cover Painting and Drawings by Silvana Waniuk
Typeset in Tahoma and Goudy Old Style
Designed by Valentine Narvey

True culture and worship are one, not in any limited sectarian or formal sense, but essentially. True culture is the expression of an inner feeling that has been brought to life, and is closely related to self-knowledge and the realization of a person's true talent, made possible by the practice of the latihan.

Muhammad Subuh Sumohadiwidjojo, Wolfsburg, 1972

ACKNOWLEDGMENTS

I am deeply indebted to Honey Thomas who encouraged and assisted me in the early stages of the book. A big thank you goes to Anthony Bright-Paul for his magnificent Foreword; to Ilaina Lennard for her proofreading; and to Harris Smart for publishing selections of the book in Subud Voice. Valentine Narvey receives special thanks for having taken on the book design and much else. I thank Gordon Campbell and all the friends who read the manuscript, or parts of it, for their comments and encouragement. My final thanks go to my husband and daughter for their unqualified support during the many years it has taken me to write this book.

For Ilana

CONTENTS

FOREWORD

Why does anybody come to the Brotherhood of Subud? And how do they find their way there in any case? Particularly since the founder of Subud, Pak Subuh, made it abundantly clear that, 'Experience first, explanations later.' To the Western mind this is an incomprehensible order of things.

So we have to go back further. Why do men, or at least some men and women look for the meaning of Life? Why this inner compulsion – which has sometimes been called 'magnetic centre' – to seek for an answer to this fundamental question, which will not go away and is impossible to solve?

It may well be that the Prophets of the great Religions of the World have already answered this question. Unfortunately most often the words and the counsels of the Founders have been misunderstood by their disciples; it cannot be otherwise. In consequence all the great religions that should be absolutely in accord with one another are at daggers drawn, each religion claiming that theirs' is the unique and sole receptacle of Truth.

Ask any priest, imam or rabbi, what is the meaning of life, and they will give you a set of regulations, a catechism of beliefs. Modern man is unable to accept regulations, particularly from those who show that they are only too human themselves. And as for Belief, its very nature is questioned. Who, in the persona, is believing and what exactly is believed? For man has a multiplicity of 'I's, and the Real Self or his real 'I' is not present. The difficulty for modern man is that he cannot believe anything unless it is a fact of his experience.

Now that man has travelled into space, now that man can Google the Universe and look at Planet Earth from afar, now that he is discovering every day new universes millions of light years away, the old conceptions of a God sitting up somewhere in the clouds surrounded by Seraphim and Cherubim no longer hold water. However, far from God being destroyed by modern science, even an elementary understanding of the laws of physics, biology or physiology compels in us all a feeling of awe and wonder at the incredible complexity of nature. This profound appreciation of Great Nature is at the base of a true religious feeling, and that is something that is shared by millions, whatever they may consider themselves, agnostic or even atheist. In that sense millions of people are fundamentally religious.

So there are those who wish to find the Way; who keep asking what is the road to Eternal Life? What is the reason for our individual and our collective lives on this Planet? Does each one of us have a 'blueprint' that is to say an individual 'pattern of possibilities' (Pace J.G. Bennett) or will we all be melted in one huge pot, like Ibsen's button moulder?

Such seekers for answers to life's conundrums very often cannot find satisfaction in orthodox religions, and look for other ways. Perhaps the best known of these are the various forms of Yoga where yoga means union with God. In Islam there are the mystical movements of the Dervishes and in Buddhism there are the Zen Masters. In all these disciplines a Teacher is necessary, a Guru or a Master; that is a human being who undertakes to show other human beings the answers to the mysteries of the universe. These ways are sometime called the 'tariqat', to distinguish them from the religions of observances and regulations.

Perhaps the most famous of these Teachers in modern times is the renowned Georgy Ivanovich Gurdjieff, whose teaching and methods were elucidated majestically by P.D. Ouspensky in his magnum opus, *In Search of the Miraculous*. Gurdjieff called his methods the Fourth Way, since they required the pupils to remain in normal life, unlike the other ways, which call for retirement to a monastery or a *tekke*, or to remote forest places. The Gurdjieff methods required a Teacher and indeed have spawned many would-be teachers, as the late J.G. Bennett, Madame de Salzmann, Dr Kenneth Walker, and others.

None of these followers were of the same stature as Gurdjieff himself, though all were remarkable people. And although these quite famous people in their own right attempted to carry on 'The Work' as it came to be known, none of them professed to have the knowledge and charisma of the founder.

So we come to the year 1957, when a movement called Subud, an acronym of *Susila, Budhi, Dharma*, appeared here in the Western world. A certain Husein Rofé had been to Indonesia and was the first

Westerner to be initiated into the *latihan kejiwaan* of Subud, the training or the spiritual exercise of Subud. Through his writings in various journals, it came to the notice of a number of followers of Ouspensky that something extraordinary was happening in Indonesia.

Husein Rofé was the first to carry Subud outside of Indonesia, and himself 'opened' people first in Japan, Hong Kong and Cyprus before finally arriving in England. It was there that he opened first of all such old Ouspenskeyites as Baron Ronimund von Bissing, Aubrey Wolton, Reginald Hoare, and eventually John Godolphin Bennett himself.

Once these old pupils of The Work had received and experienced the latihan for some months, they asked Husein Rofé to invite the founder of Subud, Pak Subuh, on their behalf to come to England. It should be noted here that not one of these pupils of Gurdjieff's methods had had any previous contact with Pak Subuh. Their interest had been aroused solely by their experience of the latihan itself. They felt sure that this spiritual exercise leads to the Awakening of that Conscience to which Gurdjieff had referred, as being the one Sacred Impulse that had not been distorted or atrophied, being buried deeply in the essence of man, within the sub-conscious.

So it came about that in the spring of 1957 Pak Subuh came to England accompanied by his wife, Ibu, his daughter, Rahayu, and two helpers, Icksan and Ismana, and was invited to stay in Coombe Springs, a large country house set in acres of grounds, close to Kingston-on-Thames, which was Bennett's Headquarters.

Now nothing so far has been said of Pak Subuh, the founder of Subud. As a young man he was also a Seeker of the Truth, sitting at the feet of various *kyai*, all of whom refused to instruct him, feeling that he was already at a stage where God alone could be his teacher. In *Concerning Subud*, by J.G. Bennett, the first book to be published on the subject of Subud, after *The Path of Subud* by Husein Rofé, Bennett writes:

> 'In Muhammad Subuh's twenty-fourth year, he had the first of a series of remarkable experiences that led to his final understanding of his mission in life. One night in the summer of 1925, he was walking in the open under a moonless sky, when he saw high above his head a ball of brilliant light that seemed brighter than the

noonday sun. While he was wondering about the meaning of this apparition, the light itself descended and entered him through the crown of his head, filling his body with radiance. The vibrations produced in his body and feelings by this experience were the first intimation of the working of the spiritual exercises, which later were to be known by the name of Subud. That the apparition of the ball of light was not a subjective hallucination peculiar to himself is indicated by the fact that many friends in the town and even many miles away also saw it and came the next morning to his house to enquire what had happened. On subsequent occasions, others, especially his mother, witnessed the same phenomena as him and often could verify and amplify his own descriptions.'

As Bennett had a large number of followers of 'The Work' throughout the world, it was his intention at first to ask only a number of specially 'prepared' people to be opened. He had reckoned without Pak Subuh, though, who said that anyone who asked could be opened. So Bennett had to explain Subud not only to his own pupils but also to many other followers of diverse esoteric methods. I say 'explain' but this is the wrong word. Because Bennett did not and could not explain Subud, but he could explain the dilemma of all enquiring people, what he himself in a former book had described as 'The Crisis in Human Affairs'; with the result that some 400 people of all ages and of many different religions elected to be 'opened' in the following months.

Why 'opened'? Because it is said that Subud is the 'awakening of the soul'. Because man is 'closed' by his imaginings, his daydreams, and his incessant desires, which though useful for his daily life, can be a hindrance to his receiving guidance from higher sources beyond his functions. Certainly we are bound by material forces and are subject as never before to all sorts of suggestions emanating from television and the media, so that it is difficult to distinguish the truth, let alone one's own truth.

But what was and is different in Subud? Why is it said that it is a receiving rather than a teaching? Why is it not a teaching, and why does it not require a Teacher, cum Guru, cum Master? Pak Subuh was as good as his word. He gave explanations only to people who had already been opened, who already had some experience. In the latihan everyone receives individually and is moved not by an instruction, as for example in the Sacred Dances that Gurdjieff taught his pupils, but each individual receives their own training from their own 'Inner Teacher'. That is what distinguishes Subud from any other method.

One can imagine the devastating effect that such an experience lead to. As every single person has their own unique experience, there is no longer any need for a leader. Within three months many of those who were opened at Coombe Springs were not only exercising on their own in local groups, but as some became a little more adept, or received more clearly, they were made Helpers and were given permission to open others. Thus the pupils of Bennett, however much they respected him as their former Teacher, once established in the latihan kejiwaan had no further need of him. Nor did they need Husein Rofé, whose role diminished as Subud spread to Europe, Asia, the Americas and Australasia, which it did like wildfire in the decade following the arrival of Pak Subuh in England. Nor indeed did they need the physical presence of Pak Subuh himself. Though Pak Subuh was the spiritual guide to the whole movement, no one was encouraged to depend upon him personally, but upon the direction that each one received personally and severally.

All this can be read in the *History of Subud* compiled by Harlinah Longcroft and in the many books on Subud that recount the experiences of people who have been opened. So it is that now, some fifty years after Subud began in the Western World, and some twenty years since the death of Pak Subuh himself, that people are still being opened to the Subud experience all over the world. Just how does this happen? The answer is: 'Come and see for yourself.' Anyone who sincerely wishes to can be opened, after a brief period to think it over, so that the decision is theirs alone. What is so wonderful is that Buddhists and Hindus, Shintoists and Confucians, Jews, Christians and Muslims, all do the spiritual exercises together, without departing from the religion of their birth, and indeed very often with a profounder understanding of it.

That such a dispensation should occur in these turbulent times is truly remarkable. Here is a short extract from a talk by Pak Subuh at Eindhoven, Holland, October 4th 1957.

'There are many human beings who attempt by various ways to reach a state in which they may become able to receive the gift of God, by stilling their hearts and their minds, for such is the state or condition in which alone a man is able to receive Divine Grace. It is therefore quite extraordinary, and ought to amaze us, that we, in a state which is by no means of this kind, are yet able to receive the gift from Almighty God as we have received it in the latihan.'

Silvana Waniuk's book is an eloquent witness to the power of the latihan, to the power that brings about an inner transformation; to a belief in a Higher Will that comes not from a Teaching or a Creed, but from a personal experience of the Great Life Force.

Anthony Bright-Paul
Author, My *Stairway to Subud*
December 16, 2008

PART ONE
BEIT-YITZHAK

Prelude

April 1964. It was the last day of the voyage. The Turkish ship was due to enter the Marseilles harbour in two hours. Already the passengers had said their good-byes, casual friendships melting into indifference. All stood on deck to watch the approaching land but I headed down to the deserted lounge. If only I could prolong indefinitely this hermetic, floating existence. For in truth, I was not travelling for pleasure or study, but had left Israel in desperation, running away from my life.

Settling down into an easy chair I noticed that I was not alone. In the far corner sat a young man playing softly on his guitar oblivious to the world. I could hear fragments of a Bach prelude – so he too played the classical guitar. Throughout the voyage he kept fiercely to himself but now, with nothing to lose, I dared an imposition. And thus, in the short time left before the ship docked, we forged the quick and intense friendship of travellers everywhere, be it on ship, plane, or train. We parted with regret, we shall never meet again. He headed to the highway to hitchhike and I, with my guitar and heavy suitcases, waited for the slow night train to London.

The train was packed. I had to stand in the crowded aisle, and that's how I spotted among the sitting passengers this young man who, for a split second, I took to be my new friend from the ship. The resemblance was remarkable. He had the same features and colouring, the same bushy eyebrows, and his sleek black hair fell over his forehead in exactly the same manner. However, the guitarist had the pinched and intense look of a very private person, while this fellow was handsome and surrounded by friends. I didn't dare approach him – maybe later…

He didn't get off in Paris and when, after boarding the boat in Calais, he stood in my line of non-British passport holders, I resolved to act – it was now or never.

I came over boldly, 'Excuse me, you remind me of somebody.' I coloured; what a lame opening. 'Are you an American?'

His expression confirmed my fears.

'Yes,' he barely deigned me a look.

'Are you from Chicago?'

Taken aback, 'Yes?'

'Do you have a brother by the name of Thomas?'

Yes!'

'Did your brother recently finish his studies in law; does he play classical guitar, and has he been travelling in Israel?'

Yes, he had, and indeed I was talking to Thomas's younger brother, who grudgingly told me that they hadn't heard from Thomas for months and that his parents were beginning to worry. Stammering nervously I related to him my conversation with Thomas, what he had done and what he was planning to do. Then my mission accomplished, feeling terribly awkward, I slunk back to my place in line, hoping to be swallowed by the crowd.

Two brothers who had been in Marseilles on the same day, who could have met but didn't; and I, a stranger, had been assigned to be a link between them. Surely this was not a coincidence!

For years I marvelled, why me?

Now, forty years later, I believe I understand. There was irony in that encounter. I wasn't a believer then, nor in the habit of meditating on existential questions, yet in one of the more chaotic and pointless moments of my life I was made to witness a higher order, an infinitesimal fraction of that web of vibrating and connecting threads that holds our lives and the universe. It was a promise, I would not be lost.

This story came up as I was planning the book and searching for a format that would be other than chronological. Its apparent arbitrariness reminded me that when I look at my life I tend to perceive it as a set of unconnected events in which the present and the past intermingle continuously. I believe that some of these events are preordained and imagine them as strategic dots on an invisible blueprint. And this is how I will proceed, drawing lines between seemingly disparate stories – not unlike that childhood game of joining numbered dots on paper. Perhaps after I have connected the most prominent ones, a new understanding will emerge.

But why write this book in the first place? After all I haven't made a name for myself and can boast of no great achievements. And though I may have had a rather eventful life, it wouldn't have been a good enough reason for writing this book if it weren't for Subud. I have been a member of the spiritual association of Subud for nearly four decades, and it has been a profound journey of self-discovery and growth. It is this that I am compelled to write about.

Yet I am not a writer, but a musician and a painter. My first languages are Hebrew and German, not English. I wouldn't have dared to attempt this venture if it weren't for a persisting inner prompting to get on with it! Thus, with trepidation and with the hope that I will be helped along the way, I begin my story.

The Watershed

The watershed of my life, the great divide that separated that which had been from what was to come – for all the remaining days of my life – happened on the day I joined Subud and received the contact with the Great Life Force. In other words when I was *opened* and began to follow the *latihan kedjiwaan* – the spiritual training of Subud. This was my personal Exodus, my Crossing of the Red Sea, my receiving the Covenant. The date was February 11, 1970.

Momentous as the experience was, my initial introduction to Subud was anything but auspicious. Five years earlier I received a letter from my friend Josepha in London, in which she informed me that her life had taken an unexpected turn, that she had joined a spiritual brotherhood called Subud, that she had met there her future husband, and that she had found what she had been searching for. She ended the letter saying that she believed Subud was 'just the thing' for me, and hoped that I would be interested. She would gladly send me more information.

But I wasn't interested in the least. Spiritual matters of any kind were not on my agenda. I had just returned from England and was in the process of establishing myself as a classical guitar teacher in Jerusalem. At the age of 27, with a number of aimless years behind me, I wanted stability above all else. Yet as my friend's letter couldn't be ignored, and in order to please her, I asked for the information. A package arrived promptly containing a thin volume, *The Meaning of Subud* by Muhammad Subuh, and a leaflet, *A First Introduction to Subud* by Roseanna Sawrey-Cookson. I could read neither – both the book and the leaflet were incomprehensible. So I let it be; if it made Josepha happy, all the better, but there was nothing in it for me.

How I subsequently came to Subud will be told later. Allow me here to fast forward to 1973. By now I have gone through an extraordinary time, and am in the midst of a so called 'Subud crisis': intent on ridding myself, as much as it is possible, of any 'incriminating' evidence from the past. I sift through piles of detritus, ripping up old diaries, letters, photos and artwork – a total purge. Suddenly, in the middle of this manic activity, a feeling of peace descends on me. Randomly I pick up a diary. It is dated 1965. Leafing through it, I cringe – ugh, such heavy, whiny stuff. Then one entry catches my eye: written in a deliberate hand, it is a recording of a dream. As I read on, the memory of the dream washes over me like a powerful wave, as vivid and fresh as if I'd woken up from it a moment ago.

I am in a spacious park, in the company of my brother Stephan and his wife Hanna. We are standing on the bank of a fast-flowing river. It is a clear bright spring day. A picturesque wooden bridge spans the river. On the other side, on the grassy bank there stands a white marquee and a crowd of people in festive dress is milling about it. I turn to Stephan and say (in Hebrew): 'I am going to cross the river to receive spiritual enlightenment; will you join me?'

Stephan declines. Hanna seems to want to come, but hesitates and stays behind. I walk purposefully across the bridge and approach the tent. At the entrance I am greeted by a stately, dark man. To my surprise, he is not wearing the expected saffron-coloured robe, but an elegant European suit. He offers me his hand, which feels large and light and full of life, and says smiling, in English, 'welcome.'

I remember how astonished I was when I awoke. The dream was so vibrant, unlike any I had ever had. But more surprising was its content. For I had never searched for spiritual enlightenment – such words were simply not in my vocabulary. Amused I thought that someone 'the Sandman' had made a mistake and that this dream wasn't meant for me! I also remember how immediately I wrote it down, recording the time (4:00 a.m.) and how, promptly, I went back to sleep. It was completely forgotten in the morning.

Sitting on the floor surrounded by torn paper, I am overwhelmed and cry with wonder. I had a dream about Bapak and Subud when I had yet to learn of their existence! It was proof that my coming to Subud had been preordained; that it wasn't I who had chosen Subud, but that Subud had chosen me.

And I did find Josepha's old letter; it had survived the purge. She didn't date it, but there was a postmark on the envelope. The letter was mailed on the day I had the dream – it had to be so; it was a perfectly crafted sign.

Spring in Berlin

In a postcard from Lichtenrade, Berlin, to his sister, Margarete Tornowsky Pinner, in Palestine, my father announces my birth:

'Yesterday, Friday, May 13, (1938), at 4:00 p.m., she came into the world, Magdalena Elisabeth, unwilling but healthy. It wasn't easy, but mother too is hale and beaming.'

I have it still, thin and yellowed, written in illegible Gothic script. But only now I notice the airmail stamp – representing a rising sun with a Swastika on its face, and an eagle sweeping over the world, its wings covering half the globe.

As I began writing about my early life I found the going heavy. The story is loaded and there is no simple way in which to tell it. It was then that my paintings came to mind. Why not use them as prompters, like objects in a show and tell presentation? It is for that reason that the headings of the next few chapters are titles of paintings; thus also 'Spring in Berlin'.

This particular painting was based on a photograph of my father and me, a six-week-old baby, smiling lovingly into each other's eyes. My aim was to convey the initial bonding between the elderly father and his radiantly smiling baby, but then I also addressed what the camera lens didn't catch, namely the evil beyond the nursery, the fear, the fatalism, the burden on my father's shoulders to save the family, but also his renewed hope and our eventual escape.

We left Germany in the nick of time, on August 28, 1939, four days before the outbreak of the war; my parents, my brother Stephan (who was just turning 16) and I, going via Trieste to Palestine. My eldest brother, Hanania, did not come with us. He had left the previous year for England, there to study pottery.

Stephan told me that on the train they swung a hammock across the seats for me, and that I was miserable throughout the journey. According to him the silver lining was that even though the train was crowded, passengers shunned our compartment because of the crying baby. It seemed to have amused my family but I was never quite sure; I didn't relish the thought of being left fretting in a precarious hammock, driving people away. I was also told that the journey unsettled me so that I regressed and stopped talking or walking unaided for a long time; I started to talk again only by the age of three.

We stayed for a few months at my aunt's place in Tel-Aviv while Stephan apprenticed for a farmer, learning about growing vegetables and raising chickens, while my parents prepared to join up with a group of homesteaders who intended to settle on the land.

The new settlement was to be a co-op village, or Moshav. It was named Beit-Yitzhak, to honour the philanthropist Yitzhak Feuerring, whose widow donated the money for its support.

Beit-Yitzhak is located in the centre of the country, 5 kilometres east of Netanya. In 1939 it was a wasteland of sand dunes. The settlers were all middle-class German Jews, many approaching middle age. They were unaccustomed to physical work and struggled with primitive conditions, with shortages, and with the intense heat. But they were determined, motivated, and highly organized. Beit-Yitzhak became a thriving place. My father, however, didn't live to see it in its glory. He died in 1947, one year before Israel's declaration of independence.

A Common Tragic Flaw

Both my parents were disciples of the German Jewish philosopher Constantin Brunner (1862-1937). My mother, Rosalia or Rozka (pronounced Rooshka), was born in 1906, in Krakow, Poland; she was the youngest of four. Her father, Shmuel Fischer, was a pious Yeshiva scholar. Her mother, Feigel died when Rozka was eleven and Rozka was subsequently raised by her eldest sister, Malka.

Rozka excelled in school, went to university and obtained a doctorate in Latin and German literature (it was there that she came across the writing of Constantin Brunner). She became a teacher in a Jewish gymnasium for girls. As for religion, she said she officially severed her ties with Judaism, at the age of 18, when she stopped fasting on Yom Kippur.

My father, Ernst Ludwig Pinner, was born in 1889 in Kosten, which was then part of Germany. He was the eldest of three. His father, Sigismund Pinner, was a lawyer who came from an assimilated Jewish background. His mother, Elisabeth, was an educated, serious woman who quietly held on to her faith. In his youth Ernst joined the Zionist movement but later he found the answers to his spiritual quest in the philosophy of Spinoza and Constantin Brunner. He served in the army during the First World War and was wounded fighting on the eastern front. After the war he finished his studies in law, married Frieda Bielschowsky, and settled in Lichtenrade, a rural suburb of Berlin.

Frieda died in 1934, leaving Ernst with two young boys, Stephan and Hanania, aged 11 and 13. It was Brunner who played the matchmaker by introducing Ernst, his favourite disciple, to Rozka, his young Polish protégé. As the political situation didn't permit easy border crossing, Ernst and Rozka met in a Czech border town in the mountains. Rozka arrived to their first meeting with a cast on her leg – not conducive for a romantic encounter. But she was young and bright and captured Ernst with her spunk and humour. Shortly after, in the spring of 1936, they got married.

Imagine then this young intellectual woman, who was accustomed to a rather bohemian lifestyle, marrying this charming but much older man, who by all accounts was an awe-inspiring personality; leaving behind her family and friends and her beloved Poland, to go to Nazi Germany, there to take over his exacting Prussian household, assume the role of stepmother to his two teenage boys, and shortly after also take in his recently bereaved father. Add to that her want of basic housekeeping knowledge and lack of female support and you see that, although she was very brave, something was bound to give.

My father wrote:

'The workload on Rozka is truly too great…That R. had to take over the two sons was natural. That our old father had to join us was unavoidable; and it is most recommendable that R. cares for all this without any signs of unwillingness. Now the child has arrived as well, requiring 5 hours of care daily …even now R. doesn't complain; but I can see that it is beyond her strength.'

To put it plainly, I was too much. There survived a coloured photo from 1939. My mother and I are posing for the camera; she is supporting me and holding my hand, but there is no embrace, no warmth, and no apparent bond. We look like two polite, slightly awkward acquaintances.

Later, as a child of three or four, I could be found alone anywhere in Beit-Yitzhak; along the sandy roads, the *wadis*, or out in the fields. Was it because I loved to roam in the outdoors, or were these symptoms of a child emotionally detached from her mother, or both? My mother used to summon me home with a shrill singsong call: '*Magdalenchen – komm nachhause – Leah, Leah, Leah!*' (Leah was the dog.) Her call could be heard all over the village and was mimicked by everyone. I didn't mind the teasing – it was mostly good-natured; but I remember being terribly embarrassed on her account.

I heard this anecdote in my teens. The visiting grandmother of a friend recalled an incident from our early childhood, how my friend, coming home one day from playing outside, stood in the doorway announcing pompously: 'Today is Shabbat, therefore today we will not beat up little Magdalenchen!' The old woman chuckled gently, and my friend and I laughed dutifully, but I was stunned; was this true? I had no recollection of being abused by other children. But I believed the story. It was a strange confirmation of something barely acknowledged – that when I was very small I was quite an abandoned little girl.

My mother was a small woman with an engaging open face, lively intelligent eyes and a ruddy complexion that gave her a youthful appearance. She didn't put on airs and was tolerant and liberal – though she didn't suffer fools gladly. She never gossiped and was loyal to her friends, who were many. She was an outgoing person with a childish charm but also, like a child, she lacked insight and self-awareness. Those who loved her were amused by her shortcomings, and she too was able to laugh at herself, which was endearing. But it was different between mother and daughter. Coming from a different mould (I resemble my father), and being an introvert with an overdose of self-awareness, I was like a stranger to her; she never understood me and, conversely I became increasingly critical and embarrassed by everything about her person.

No doubt I received from her ample intellectual stimulation. She taught me to read music and read and write in German, she read to me from Grimm's fairytales to Thomas Mann and Rilke, she took me to concerts and the theatre, and we talked about books, films and ideas. But in the realm of the feelings the winds blew sharp and dry, and when it rained it came down like a cloudburst with sheets of water and pelting hail.

Soon after my father died I became the target of her discontent; I was a mediocre student who would never measure up to her who had always been at the top of her school; I was lazy and didn't work as hard as our neighbour's son, who loved and helped his widowed mother; in short I was an overall disappointment. However, already from the age of five I

12

was given tasks which, as I grew older, became a growing list of daily chores: to sweep the floor, wash the dishes, make the beds, darn my socks, collect the eggs, feed the chicken, de-tick the dogs, do my laundry and what not. This was accompanied by incessant nagging and shouting... she couldn't let me be, I had to look busy at all times. And because of her attitude, and because she told me so, I grew up believing myself incapable of achieving anything of worth, that I had no chance of following in my parents' footsteps, and that basically, I was good for nothing.

Life in our household of two, after we had moved to a new house, leaving the farm to Stephan, centred on her person and her complains. In fact our roles were reversed. It was I who was expected to give her support and sympathy – something which I was not able to do. As I headed into my later teens, her tantrums became a frequent occurrence. I learned to cope with them (you let the anger wash over you without resistance, like diving under a breaker, until it loses its momentum), but it meant that I was constantly on the alert; I never knew when and why a storm would hit me.

Of course I was aware of her many difficulties and disappointments; that she was by nature high-strung and suffered from repeated illnesses, real and imaginary. But would I have been able to forgive her had I loved her, or if she had asked my forgiveness after one of her, often inexplicable and unprovoked, tempers? It is a hypothetical question. Being a child, I never question *her* love but I have one distinct memory from when I was twelve, how, in a sudden flash of recognition I knew that I hated her from the very core of my being and wanted her dead. The thought frightened me so that my hair stood on end. I knew that this was not a passing sentiment, but something real and terrible. I had finally collided with the iceberg – and this was only its tip.

Many years later, when I began to follow the spiritual training of Subud, I experienced on a deeper level the devastating ravages of this hate. I was shocked to discover that while outwardly my life was unfolding in a more or less normal fashion, inwardly I was choking in a cesspool, my inner feeling stunted in utter self-denial.

Once, on a hot summer day, on a deserted street in the outskirts of Jerusalem, I saw a black kitten that had got itself stuck in an open container of soft tar and was sinking slowly. The kitten mewed piteously, but there was no one around to help, it was too far gone, and there was nothing I could do. This was my state.

Subud is about change and I wanted so badly to become a better person. Yet no matter how much I strove, it was out of my hands. This inner negativity couldn't be pulled out like a bad tooth or be operated on like a ruptured appendix; and I almost lost heart. When one day I heard a silent voice that was accompanied by a wondrous feeling of compassion; 'You shall need a lifetime of prayer, if not more, before you'll see a change.' In other words, the healing I was hoping for will take a long time. Not a cheery thought, yet pragmatic. Therefore I'd better stop agonizing and picking at my wounds, but keep following the spiritual training of Subud, surrender everything to the Almighty and live my life the best I can.

My daughter Ilana was born on May 27, 1980. I was in a small rural hospital in Canada, and had been a long time in labour. At times I felt terribly alone, as if abandoned – my husband was at work and the nurses joked that the family doctor had gone fishing. As the first day drew to an end I remembered: this was the anniversary of my mother's death. The baby would not, could not, arrive today. Only twenty-four hours later, when the General Surgeon made his routine visit, was the alarm raised: where was everybody? Why is this woman still in labour? The baby is in distress! Promptly a caesarean section was performed and she came into the world at 5:00 p.m. She was a large and healthy baby but her face, which was a bit puffy and red on that first day, oddly resembled my mother's. The likeness didn't last, but I took it as a reminder. I had been given another chance – we were given another chance.

Matryoshkas

The tiny photo I have chosen for my next project is the only other photograph I have of my father and me. In it my father is hoisting me high on his shoulder smiling to the camera, and behind us the lilac is in full bloom; probably it was taken on my first birthday. Unlike the previous painting where I aimed for a good likeness, the drawing for this one was done freely and intuitively. I liked the result, though the central figure barely resembles my father. Rather it evokes a forgotten nightmare from the time when the news of the holocaust stunned the world and my mother learned that her sister, Malka, had perished in Auschwitz.

In the dream, I am facing an emaciated child in tatters. On its skull-like head is perched an incongruous paper hat; its pale eyes are large and staring, its skin a deathly pallor, and its neck transparent as if made of glass. The child stands silent and immovable and I, paralyzed with fear, wake up screaming.

Working on the painting was slow and involved many layers of paint; but no matter what I did it would not come together. Finally, exasperated, I added impulsively a few more lines and, to my surprise, two forms materialized, the unmistakable contours of two Russian dolls or Matryoshkas. From that point the work advanced effortlessly towards its conclusion.

Matryoshkas are a set of painted wooden dolls stacked one inside the other. I had a picture of such dolls hanging over my crib. It was a coloured photograph of some toys my father had taken, one of many colour studies he had done as he upgraded his photographic skills to include colour art photography (a specialized field in those days), hoping to use it as a means to make a living for when they emigrated.

Studying the photograph with adult eyes, I notice the 'Rembrandt pallet'; gold and red against a dark-brown background. I also see a narrative; Teddy bear is the centre of the toy family, he is the Teacher. To his right stand two grimy rubber dolls – my older brothers; to his left the two Russian dolls – evidently my mother and I; at his feet are a small bear with a silver bell and a painted plastic duck – perhaps to represent music and art. One of the bear's arms is raised in a warning, prophetic gesture, the other offered gallantly to the Russian doll. Only Bear survived the exodus.

But as a child I didn't like it. It was the other one I liked, a small oval picture that depicted a grandmother knitting by an open window through which could be seen the edge of a garden, a church spire and the sky; while the whole unseen town was reflected in its glass pane! It was that miraculous reflection of the unseen world that caught my soul. By comparison, the photo of my toys was oddly oppressive. The rubber dolls were ordinary and the bear was just my old familiar bear. The Russian dolls, however, were a different matter. To begin with, I was told that they had been mine, which was disconcerting since they were beyond memory. I regretted terribly not having them; they were so elegant in their painted red, gold and purple costumes. There was also the maddening question: how many more dolls were hidden in those two and did they get smaller ad infinitum? But then, beyond it all there lay something even more disturbing; since their image was a perpetual reminder of all that we had lost: the family effects, our beautiful home, the life we had had, and our family's true identity. They stood for my lost Paradise.

Among my notes I found this entry, dated April 4, 2001.
'I had a dream in which I am carrying a little girl on my shoulders, and I must go back to Beit-Yitzhak. But I don't want to return and begin to cry; it is too painful. It is a place where I have no identity and no potential; where there is no future, only hidden despair. Yet I miss it, as it is beautiful...

'Most likely the dream is an answer to the question: why paint this heavy subject. Thinking about it I get all tangled up. Am I the child on my shoulders – as on my father's shoulder? But this child is older, a chubby six-year-old, leaning heavily on my head, partially covering my eyes and hampering my progress.

'Later I think that maybe I, the toddler in the photo, in loving my father, have taken into my soul my father's burden, which is weighing me down... But now I am in a real pretzel: I carry the child on my shoulders; the child is I; the child is my father – the father that I the child internalized. Therefore, the image of my father lifting me is inverted in the dream, to indicate that now it is I who is carrying my father.

'Too complicated,
But it makes sense...'

Nobody in our family ever talked about the history of our survival. I learned about it many years later. Then I discovered the disconcerting truth that it could have ended very badly indeed. That my father, this wise and proud man, had been caught, and was almost defeated, by a crippling inertia that held him back from doing anything to save himself and his family, until it was almost too late.

I learned that, to begin with, in 1925, under Constantin Brunner's influence, Ernst left the Zionist movement and, with Brunner's encouragement, but against the explicit wishes of his wife, his sister and his friends, he published a paper renouncing Zionism. In it he argued that the Zionist mandate to re-build the land of Israel was not feasible and the wrong solution for the Jewish people. He believed that the Jews were the indisputable and legitimate citizens of the country in which they resided. He saw himself as a German of Jewish descent, with no split loyalty. Germany was his homeland!

Thus when the Nazis came to power in 1933, when his sister and many of his friends, artists and intellectuals, had already left or were leaving Germany he wrote:

17

'I watch the situation here with growing pessimism. Anti-Semitism has become a surrogate religion and is fanned by a new fanaticism and new beliefs. It is the religion of negativity. The image of the Jew (as the absolute negative, the devil…) is being placed alongside the hazy image of one's marvellous race (the absolute positive), which means that this "god" can only exist as an opposition to the devil; it has no existence without it. And how else can this god be served and brought offerings but by out-rooting the devil?'

But even in the face of a looming war, of total isolation and the ever-tightening restrictions on Jewish life, which had affected him directly, when Jewish lawyers were barred from practicing law and his sons banned from higher education, Ernst still vacillated and procrastinated.

As late as 1938 he wrote:

'You know, I don't let myself get agitated anymore with every new event. The worst is already here: the world is going under and one cannot counter it. I cannot foresee if I'll be among the 25% that will perish or among the 75% that will survive…And it is the same to me if I live 10 more years or die today. Not because I scorn life…I love it, but I love much more than merely living.

'Certainly I shall get out when it will become unbearable. Exile cannot be worse than the present situation. Thus I will go with the very last, following the rhythm of my nature, whether praiseworthy or censured…this is who I am, this is what I have been apportioned.

'Want, misery, hate, friendship, they are to be found everywhere; and everywhere there is Love, and everywhere there is Eternity…

The day of my departure has not yet arrived…'

But my coming into the world had changed something, and the prospect of immigrating to Palestine became more realistic. From a letter dated June 30, 1938.

'Yes, I am in such a situation that I want to get out…I welcome the thought of Palestine. Your description of an egg-producing village kindles my imagination – a simple life of hard work in the realm of the most basic of production – I'd prefer that, provided my body can withstand it. I cannot see myself doing much else in Palestine. Above all not photography which is such a city luxury…'

In a letter from November 17, 1938, after the ominous events of the Kristallennacht Pogrom, he writes:

'I believe that in a few months we will be with you. The thought makes me very happy. And when in these terrible times I might have lost my grip for a moment, believe me that now I give the sobbing free rein and allow myself to dream. I know that it will be very difficult, but it will be also beautiful. When I think that once again I will be among free people rejoicing in song…

'When I wrote regarding USA, Ecuador, Australia, there always stood behind the question why not Palestine? Therefore today I have no reservation, no hesitations, no re-thinking. There is no going back from this YES…'

***

My earliest memories of Beit-Yitzhak are of nights when I was left alone in the house, my parents and Stephan gone to one of their many meetings, and awake in bed I would listen to the jackals in the fields, their haunting calls so close and blood chilling. There was rustling in the honeysuckle by the window. Was it a mouse or a fadaiyun (thief)? Hiding under the blanket I'd hold my breath, petrified.

The first kindergarten in the settlement was housed in a barn on the hill near the new water tower. We were playing outside in the sand when the sirens began wailing. Italian planes were attacking the coast. The teacher, Paula, ushered us back into the barn to take shelter under the tables, but I wouldn't budge. I stood rooted to the ground and screamed at the empty sky. I would not submit to the indignity of crawling under those silly little tables. If a bomb fell, nothing would save us anyway. I was three years old. This was my first vivid memory.

Our house was in the centre of the moshav, and our land ran in a narrow strip towards the east. It was a small house: two rooms, a bathroom, and a hallway that doubled as dining room and kitchen. At the back of the house facing the main road that traversed the village, was a small garden with a bit of lawn, avocado and clementine trees, and a flower bed. In the front grew lemon and loquat trees, which hid the chicken coops, and to the south towered the ubiquitous mulberry tree. We ate sweet mulberries on hot summer days, mulberry soup and mulberry pudding – my face, hands, and shirt eternally speckled with blue. The birds loved them too, leaving their blue calling cards on the freshly hung laundry.

We raised chickens (the moshav's mainstay) and grew vegetables. Stephan did most of the heavy work in the fields, while Ernst had his hands full with the chickens and with the operation of the village incubator, which was stationed in our barn. (I loved watching the teeming trays of newly hatched baby chicks – but why did these adorable balls of yellow fuzz, turn so quickly into such ungainly birds?) We also had some rabbits, a goat, and a bad-tempered mule we shared with the neighbour. Last but not least, there was a tabby cat, Lilly, and our many dogs – mother's hobby. And though the dogs had a proper kennel, they all lived happily with us in the house, puppies, ticks, fleas and whatnot. My father said that he wouldn't mind being a dog in the Pinner household, well fed, well loved, and sleeping long hours in the shade.

Our family seemed ordinary enough, eking a living from the land like everybody else – but we were not. Despite the endless chores and the debilitating heat, my parents continued their lifelong spiritual and intellectual persuit.

My father wrote:

'Now that the long evenings are finally here, I can do some intellectual work. We read and study much Hebrew. Also I am making progress with the writings of Saint Augustine. And when this is done it will finally be the turn of Spinoza's Theological – Political Treatise, a subject that interests me greatly. It is very timely, when yet again many questions concerning the creation of a State are being weighed and no clear answers are given.'

December 9, 1944 'Everything here is as usual. There is much work on the farm, what with the incubator in full productivity ... We made some profit, oddly enough with red cabbage, not a high-end commodity, and the potato harvest was good too .... My lecture in Tel-Aviv will take place in January. I have put much effort into it and am almost done. I teach two courses [in B-Y] in which I read and give commentary on the Ethics. And though the material is difficult, none has given up as yet ... Much time is spent in Hebrew classes and the many meetings; e.g. in this week alone five evenings were taken.'

May 22, 1946 '... In any case I am not a fanatical adherent to Brunner's teaching and feel a kinship with all who experience and live their inner Oneness, whatever their path. For myself, for my intellectual cleanliness, there is only that of Spinoza and Brunner, but there are, likewise, other roads that lead to the Oneness, and thus to Amor Dei.

I only ask that you let yourself be helped. In our cultural climate, when most people are afflicted by the illness of modern scepticism, few can achieve it on their own.'

I would watch him coming up the path, after tending the chickens, looking worn out, his bald head gleaming with sweat, the sunset reflected in his glasses. I revered him, but stayed out of his way. After supper he'd retire to the study, light a pipe, the tobacco fragrance filling the house, and sit at his desk to study, read, or write; he was not to be disturbed. He surrounded himself with beautiful things. There stood in the corner the crank-up phonograph and a small collection of records – Handel, Bach, and Mozart. On his desk stood a framed photograph of Constantin Brunner and on the walls hung reproductions of Raphael,

Leonardo, Durer, Picasso, and one real painting, a copy of a Van der Wyden, 'Portrait of a Woman'; the pale lady with the white headdress whose solemn eyes follow you everywhere. There were many books, and we had also, behind glass, a luxurious, albeit slightly chipped, set of fine gold-rimmed china. This room, doubling as my parents' bedroom, was like an oasis of culture and serenity contrasting with the rest of the house which was in a perpetual state of chaos. The kitchen was my mother's domain where she ruled with her loud voice and energetic bustle; and Stephan and I shared the second room, my odd collection of toys encroaching on his side and his dirty boots and smelly socks flung onto mine.

But gradually an undetected sadness took hold of my heart because, with all his work and intellectual activity, my father had little time for me, his youngest. I have scarcely a handful of memories of time shared with him. Being carried from the bath, wrapped in a large white towel, and riding on his knees to the German singsong *Hope hope Reiter* (shrieking with delight when the rider falls into the *Sumpf*). I was older and had become quite the chatterbox; we always had lively conversations around the dinner table and I still see his mounting irritation until he'd snap, 'Hold your tongue and let the grownups talk.'

And then there was the time he raised his hand to me. I must have been five. I got into the sugar bowl (I was a sugar junkie) and to hide my misdeed, those were rationing times, I replenished the bowl with a white crystalline substance I found in the bottom of the kitchen cupboard, which happened to be Naphthalene. I hid in my room behind the door, listening to the family sitting down for afternoon tea, waiting for the anger of the gods to erupt. No word was heard, only the violent scraping of a chair; then the door flung open and wordlessly he yanked me from behind and slapped me across the face.

This is the bulk of my memories. It seems to me that I had been losing him by degrees long before he died.

In the spring of 1947 my father was diagnosed with cancer and, after an unsuccessful operation, brought home to die. He needed regular morphine shots, yet towards the end he refused the drug; he wanted to be lucid in his last hours.

And when did my mother find the time and energy to teach me that spring to read and write in German? On my father's birthday, a month before his death, I presented him with a special gift: a letter in German, written in a large, childish, ornate hand. He sat on the veranda in the afternoon shade, reclining in an easy chair. I watched him read the letter, his face pale and withdrawn, but in his blue eyes there was a twinkle.

During the last stages of his illness I was packed away to stay with neighbours. It was a very long summer in exile. They had two children, a girl my age and a boy of four. The good thing was that my friend had toys like nobody else's, dolls with eyes that opened and shut, an exquisite little grocery store, a proper swing, and a dress-up tickle-trunk. We had fun despite the mother who was everything my mother was not: a fussy housewife who kept up appearances and controlled her family with an iron fist. She made me feel like an intruder and treated me with subtle hostility, as if I was a threat to herself or her daughter. She laid traps for me; I had to prove myself, for wasn't I the daughter of Ernst and Rozka Pinner, those intellectuals? She'd ask me sweetly all sorts of questions, waiting for my demise. Could I identify the music on the radio? Was it a Mozart or a Haydn? Didn't I know? Why did she smile so smugly? Did she discover I was a fraud? I dreaded her friendliness worse than her bossiness. The lady visited my nightmares for years.

One day I was summoned home to say my last good-bye to Father, for the end was near. I hesitated by the door. Everything was so foreign: the sickbed, the smell, my father leaning weakly against the pillows, covered with a crumpled sheet; the house permeated with a cold sense of finality. I didn't dare enter – he was almost a stranger and I was overcome by shyness.

Years later my mother told me that on his deathbed my father regretted that his sons did not follow in his spiritual footsteps, but that he believed that it would be I who would carry his torch.

August 20, 1947 was a very hot day. My friend, her brother, and I were in the shade of the citrus orchard watering the trees, moving a water-hose from one trough to the next, making mud-pies, splashing each other, squealing with laughter. But when I saw my aunt, Tante Grete, coming up the road, trudging through the sand under a blinding midday sun, everything ceased, became suspended, and I knew that my father had died. Tante Grete, with her beautiful sad face, embraced me, and said softly, 'Come, let's go home.'

Ernst Pinner was buried the next day and people came from far and wide to pay their last respect. There were many speeches and tributes. I stood by Tante Grete, and as she held me close, I began to sob. At the time I wasn't able to feel the loss, but it was such a moving event.

The Recorder

No one questioned my musical talent, it was a given; I was the designated musical child of the family, and as proof was told, time and again, the irrefutable baby-story how, before I could even talk, I could sing from Mozart's *Eine Kleine Nachtmusik*. Another story the old kindergarten teacher loved to repeat was, how one Shabbat morning she found me, a toddler, crying in the middle of the road because I had burned my bare feet in the hot sand. When she scooped me up and asked what I was doing there, I pointed to the synagogue across on the hill, whence could be heard the sound of praying, and sobbing said, '*Singe, singe!*'

When Beit-Yitzhak became famous for its chamber music concerts, which attracted performers of the highest calibre from around the world, I was taken to all of them, self-conscious at being nearly the only child in the audience. In my teens I earned my tickets setting up the chairs in the community centre and handing out programs, and today I cannot listen to chamber music without being taken back to those concerts. For better or for worse, chamber music had become part of the fabric of my life.

There is no denying that I was blessed with certain talents: a good ear, an artistic sensitivity, moderately clever hands and a pleasant voice. I loved to sing and was a great bathroom diva, to my family's exasperation, since once I started on one of those songs with their endless stanzas, I never came out. I was also a good whistler, and often on my way home from school, farmer Adler would call after me, '*Madchen die pfeifen und Hennen die krahn, soll man beizeiten den Hals herumdrehen.*' (A whistling girl and a crowing hen always come to a bad end). Germans are not known for the subtlety of their humour. However I took it as a sort of compliment.

And don't get me wrong. I am not ungrateful for my musical gifts, but often I wondered if in different circumstances I might have been spared some of the bumpy rides I had to take in later life. For I knew that my talents as they were, were not enough, and that this supposed advantage my mother was trying to bolster, was not a true asset. I grew up with the uncomfortable knowledge that nothing was as it appeared and that basically I was a fraud.

The girl playing the recorder in the painting is a self-portrait. The photograph was taken when I was eight; yet the painting isn't about memories but about an inner state. The recorder is one of the simplest instruments to master; with only minimum instruction, anyone, child or adult, can play it tolerably well. I was a natural, and by the time I was five, when my fingers had grown long enough to cover the openings, I took to it like a fish to water. My mother and Stephan played the larger recorders, the alto and tenor, and sometimes in the evenings we would play duets and trios together. These were good times. But more often I'd play by myself, sitting on my bed tooting away at my favourite songs. At such moments it was not so much about the music or about skill as about being left alone, in an altered state, relaxed and empty – not unlike the quiet before latihan.

By the age of seven I was taken to the violinmaker Eliyahu Rapaport in Tel-Aviv and fitted with a half-size violin. I do not remember much about my first violin, but I remember Eliyahu – a kindred spirit, who became my special friend. Eliyahu was a slight and wiry man with a deeply furrowed face, a crown of wild greying hair, a gravelly voice, and one thick, overgrown, glue-encrusted thumbnail. His studio was not far from where my aunt lived and whenever we came to town to visit her, I would run over to his place.

'There you are,' he would call in a booming voice from the cavern of his workshop, 'Come in, come in.'

It was a tantalizing place. I loved the smells of wood and glue and varnishes that hit the nose upon entering; the messy workbench, the violins in their various stages of disrepair, and the gutted double bass in the corner, forever awaiting its turn. I'd perch on a high stool and he would regale me with tall tales or let me handle his prize collection of odd instruments. His favourite was the *Rebaba*, a rough, skin covered, Bedouin string instrument; mine, on the other hand, was an exquisite miniature violin with a scroll in the shape of a cherub.

These are the memories of a child. The grown-ups, I noticed, were less impressed; and when I entered my teens I began to see Eliyahu through their eyes: an eccentric, not very reliable, lonely, old man; it was sad and embarrassing, and I stopped the visits.

There is a reason why this story resurfaced; many years ago my cousin Miriam Skidan apprenticed with Eliyahu. She eventually went on to do other things, but she never lost her love for the instrument. Thus, at the age of 82, shortly before she died, Miriam, by her own initiative, raised funds among family members in Israel to help us, in Canada, buy a better violin for our musician daughter.

As for my relationship with the violin, that was a different matter. For six years I studied with Mrs. K., an elderly lady who lived in the nearby village of Nira. Daily my mother would ask, 'did you practice today?' 'Yes', I'd lie.

The violin wasn't difficult for me and I sight-read music quite easily. Why then practice? But Mrs. K. wasn't fooled; sight-reading demands intense concentration, which cannot be sustained for long and when she'd ask me to repeat something, I'd stumble and play miserably. She then would reprimand me gently and, embarrassed, I would promise to do better next time; but I seldom did. I simply didn't like the violin and dreamed of having a piano. I don't remember asking for *things* (the way children do nowadays), one simply didn't. Those were different times. But I did ask for this one thing, I wanted a piano! By the age of twelve I rebelled: piano or nothing! But my mother didn't give in; we couldn't afford one, she said, we were too poor and she wasn't going to let me abandon the music.

'How can you throw away your talents and all those years of violin playing?' she shouted, 'Not everyone is as lucky as you; do you want to end your life working as a farm labourer?' (This was her standard threat.)

At last a compromise was reached: I would continue with violin lessons, but with a new teacher, the sensational young and beautiful violinist who had come to live in our neighbourhood.

But my new teacher, Hanna B., had her own misgivings – I was in a way 'spoiled goods'; and she requested that I audition for her mentor, the violinist Lorand Fenyves. To play for this illustrious man, whom I had heard on the radio and seen on the stage in Beit-Yitzhak, with my shoddy technique and non-existent attitude, was a truly humiliating experience. And, indeed, when I left the room I overheard him sigh and say in a dismissive voice, in German, (assuming I didn't understand), 'I think she can still be saved.'

Studying with Hanna was a great improvement. I practiced daily and almost enjoyed myself. Even so, in grade twelve, after my last nervous performance in the final student concert, I called it quits and gave up the violin for good.

However that was also the time when I had to face the question I most dreaded: what was I going to do with my life? Hanna B. and my mother urged me to consider music but, notwithstanding my issues with the violin, I simply knew I wasn't good enough. The problem was that I knew of nothing else that I wanted to do. I had no ambitions and no dreams. Ironically, I only knew what I *didn't* want to do, which was to be a music teacher in schools. Our class had made the life of the music teacher, Mr. Daniel, absolute hell. To even consider such a profession was tantamount to going willingly to the gallows. Still there was little choice. What was a young woman in the fifties, in Israel, to do if she didn't get married in a hurry? She could become a secretary, a teacher or a nurse, or go to university – provided she was an outstanding scholar, which I wasn't. Thus, according to my mother, I had only two options: the Music Teacher College, or *Meshek Ha'poalot*, an agriculture college for women. The second was a threat, not a choice, so I had no choice – music teacher it was to be.

A third choice materialized in the army. In my last year of service I lived on a kibbutz. The manager of the vegetable fields offered me membership in the kibbutz and a permanent job as his assistant. He seriously believed I was throwing away a once-in-a-lifetime opportunity when I declined his offer, opting instead to study music after all.

But I needed to get away in every sense of the word. Life on the kibbutz was as narrow as in Beit-Yitzhak and worse. It was time to broaden my prospects, open my brain and widen my feelings. I might as well study music. It would be a reprieve of sorts and afterwards we shall see.

Safe Haven

Two years of army service had had no bearing on my life. Mostly it was a drab, unproductive and wasteful time. Still something like a remote chuckle reminds me that things were not what they seemed to be; that this, so called, military career of mine turned out not as expected, and that, by fluke or by decree, I was steered away to a safe haven that, to all intent and purpose, was outside army jurisdiction.

There isn't much to tell about boot camp; it was a rather lightweight affair. Making one's bed with knife-edge precision and aligning it with 15 other beds was a cinch, and I complained that we were given too much drill and not enough physical challenges. (Pre-military training in high school had been by far more demanding.) The good news was that I lost a great deal of weight. Regimented life away from the obliging fridge, and avoiding extra bread in the mess hall, did wonders; this was a first!

The Sinai War (October 1956) began just when boot camp ended. And while the whole country was caught up in the events we, the new recruits, languished forgotten in temporary camps, doing meaningless jobs, knowing and understanding little of what was going on, still wearing the obsolete recruit insignia and waiting.

Finally the day arrived. Standing at attention on the parade ground, we waited for our assignment paper; each girl secretly hoping to serve in an active unit; in the Air Force, the Commando, or the Artillery. But I was assigned to Parts and Maintenance which was on nobody's list.

Mortified yet stoical, I watched my friend and schoolmate as she walked proudly towards the group of beaming Air Force girls; and was relieved to greet as suffering companion the beautiful, self appointed queen of my class, Amira. Ah, the sweet *Schadenfreude*, how the mighty have fallen! Amira would hardly have noticed me in school; now I was her bosom-friend. And she wept on my shoulder: 'It is so unfair…Why, why?'

The course we had to take was dreadful, though I tried to look on its bright side. Where else would I learn about guns, tanks and command cars? However Amira and I were the only high school graduates among girls from very different social and ethnic backgrounds; none had education beyond grade eight; some spoke only Arabic and some were virtually illiterate. To make matters worse, we were required to attend literacy and elementary math classes, which upset Amira to such a degree that she nearly cried herself into a nervous breakdown.

At long last somebody took pity on her and we were informed – hush, hush, that we had been assigned to the unit to 'raise the overall standard' and were soon to go to an officer course. This restored Amira to her happy, haughty self, and indeed in time she would become an officer. But it wasn't to be my lot. I became very ill. The young army doctor found nothing wrong with me and said I was only shamming to shirk my duty to clean the toilet stalls. But on the weekend furlough, doubled over with pain, I hitchhiked home, where even my mother had no trouble diagnosing me with jaundice, which our doctor confirmed. The army was notified and an ambulance arrived to take me to a military hospital.

The hospital had beautiful gardens, fresh food and great company. But when I was released I had to face the absurdity that as I didn't finish the Parts and Maintenance course I had no chance for advancement and worse: I had become expendable, like a loose cog in the system. Thus I was shipped off to a garage unit 'somewhere' in the middle of the country and assigned to an office to do routine clerical work.

My boss, Miller, was a middle-aged officer, a mild man who loved to pepper every sentence with colourful swear words. Everyone knew that his bark was worse than his bite, but it was disconcerting, I was not used to such language. Miller lived in Netanya and often offered me a ride home in his jeep. One day he asked, 'Do you like working in my office?'

'So-so,' I replied.

'Why? I'm not a good officer?'

'Sure you are, but you swear too much. It doesn't become you.' I held my breath, amazed at my chutzpah.

But Miller laughed good-naturedly and, slightly embarrassed, explained, 'I have to fit in, you see.'

A few months in the army opened my eyes to see the world in a new light. In Beit-Yitzhak children were not to question adult authority – well, more or less – but by now I had shed my inborn deference and saw that there was nothing special about grownups, that on the whole they were a ridiculous sorry lot. But what impressed me more was the novelty of the awareness itself; it was like a sudden revelation, like that time, in grade six, when I tried on my mother's glasses and discovered that the tree across the road was not a hazy green blob but had distinct, sharply defined leaves.

So the time went by working in Miller's office, filling out and filing away maintenance forms. The tedium was excruciating. I began having pains in my heels and could not wear army boots. Imagine standing for morning inspection in sandals! But I met the commander's glare with defiance – I had doctor's permission.

Spring arrived. I was the only girl to represent our garage in the *Tze'adah*, the yearly national two-day Passover hike to Jerusalem. Not much else was happening: the camp had no social life; there was no one to talk to, and the only person I befriended – a civilian in his early thirties, a Russian émigré with a large moustache – fell in love with me. We hadn't even kissed, but he wanted to marry me! That was too creepy; it was time I got out of there and I asked for a transfer. I was told that it couldn't be done; our commander would never grant it; he vetoed every petition.

All the same a loophole was found – volunteering! It was a powerful means that could not be opposed. I was given two choices: to volunteer to the southernmost part of Israel, to Eilat, to serve in yet another garage, or volunteer to the NAHAL (an acronym, in Hebrew, for Combatant Pioneering Youth). The NAHAL was comprised of youth groups from various youth movements, whose ideological aim was to settle on the land. Living on a kibbutz was part of the training, as were their rigorous military exercises.

I opted for the NAHAL and my application was accepted! This was a dream come true; I was becoming part of the Israeli pioneering tradition, a step that would bestow meaning on my hitherto aimless life. I would live on a kibbutz, most likely in a new settlement in the Negev or the Galilee and fulfil another secret dream – to 'belong'.

Imagine then my disappointment when I learned that of all the kibbutzim in Israel I was to go to Ein-Gev, the kibbutz where my brother Hanania was living! I had so hoped for something new; instead I was transferred to this old, familiar place. But even then I had already a vague notion that this was not a coincidence; that 'someone' (maybe God) did 'intervene' in my life. The thought was very new – like a seed waiting to germinate; for I had never thought about God but as an abstraction which had nothing to do with me. Still whether a random chain of events, or providence, the fact remained that I was not cut out for army life. I was too young and impressionable and needed more sheltered time before joining life's roller coaster, and what safer haven to go to, but my brother's kibbutz? There I would have family support, be in the company of like-minded people, and be virtually out of army's jurisdiction. For, as it turned out, we had the bare minimum of drill, no army discipline to speak of, and we wore the uniform only when going home on leave.

At this point I should, briefly, introduce Hanania. As mentioned in an earlier chapter, Hanania had gone to England to study pottery (being a Jew he had no access to higher education in Nazi Germany). When England declared war on Germany, Hanania, like many thousands of German citizens, was interned and eventually deported to a prison camp in Australia. He was released in 1943, and upon arriving in Palestine he joined the Jewish Brigade. Eventually, after the war, he was accepted, on probation, in Kibbutz Ein-Gev. There, during the war of independence in 1948, he was severely wounded, sustaining a spinal injury that paralysed him from the waist down. After numerous operations and two years of rehabilitation he regained the partial use of his legs. At that point, sponsored by the army, he went to study at the Bezalel School of Art in Jerusalem, focusing on his chosen medium, the woodcut. Hanania then returned to Ein-Gev, married Ortrud, and remained there for the rest of his life. He worked part time teaching art and doing clerical work, but the rest of his time he devoted to his woodcuts with a single mindedness of a monk.

I had spent a few summers in Ein-Gev so that when I arrived I felt right at home. Soon, however, I realized that my fantasy to belong was just that – a fantasy. The people of the *Amirim* group, the NAHAL group I had joined, had been together since high school and army training; and though I had established a close friendship with my roommate, Ora, and though the group as a whole was friendly and outgoing, I never felt one of them. It was therefore even more important that Hanania's home was always open to me. My brother was an accommodating, quiet man with whom I could talk about anything under the sun, and his wife, Ortrud, made me feel like a princess, spoiling me rotten with her unconditional love.

Then there was the place itself. Nestled on the shore of Lake Kinneret (the Lake of Galilee), it is like a green jewel, lush with vegetation, set against the backdrop of the parched Golan-Heights, their yellow shapes so strangely alive, like the limbs of a giant monster in slumber. The view across the lake towards Tiberias is panoramic, and the lake, unique for its emotional and spiritual appeal, has a magic all of its own with its ever-changing play of light and colour, from the softest, dreamy mauves in summer, to stormy, metallic greens in winter. Summers in Ein-Gev are blisteringly hot (it is 600 feet below sea level), and in the winter a cold east wind, the Sharkia, blows down from the Heights, hitting the lake with great force like an army of demons.

Even so, I requested to work outdoors, and ended up in the vegetable fields. The work suited me. I had little dealings with people, since the vegetable fields were not popular with the *Amirim*. Few cared for the monotonous, backbreaking work, and few got along with the grumpy taciturn manager. But I was accustomed to the work from long summers in the fields of Beit-Yitzhak, and liked the man.

Primarily, however, it was about being in the outdoors. What did it matter sweating buckets among the tomato vines, being covered with revolting dust spreading chicken manure, or being assaulted by millions of bugs, if I could let the wind caress and dry my burning face, when in a moment of rest I'd inhale the clean mountain air spiced with the smells of dry grasses and hot earth, my eyes lost in the ever-changing blue expanses below? When in the ringing silence I'd catch, wafting on the wind, the faint tinkling of goat bells, Syrian goats, way up the mountain, beyond the invisible border, like black dots spilling down its yellow folds? When, after work, I'd dive into the lake like into a polished mirror…? And time would stand still.

Leaving Ein-Gev for the last time, looking back at the patchwork of fields, the receding lake and the burnt mountain, I suddenly realized that this was a final good-bye and the end of an era. I told myself not to be such a sentimental fool; I could always come back for a visit… But then a silent, inner voice spoke up and said that this year in Ein-Gev was a Gift for which I ought to give thanks! I had never experience such an inner voice before; I could feel its holiness – cool and remote like an icy spring; but as I didn't know how to pray or give thanks, I succumbed after all to maudlin sentimentality; thus with tears and a heavy heart, I bid farewell to a carefree year, I knew, would never return.

PART TWO
SUBUD

Lucia

It was recess time. Leaning against the far wall in the hallway, I watched the comings and goings. The Music Teachers' College was renting space from an elementary school in after-hours and in the corridor there still lingered the smells and echoes of running children just gone home. It has been two weeks since school began but I haven't made any effort yet to know my colleagues. At any rate we were a peculiar collection of individuals: some exceptionally talented, others appallingly mediocre; some fresh out of high school, others 'much older' in their late twenties; and, of course, those, like myself, who had come straight from the army; we had little in common.

Thus watching, I suddenly noticed a girl I hadn't seen before. She had remained in the empty classroom, sitting sideways at her desk. Her face was partially hidden behind a curtain of wavy, light-brown hair that revealed only glimpses of large eyes, full lips, and a rounded strong chin. It was a curious sensation, this seeing; like a split second of heightened reality; 'I know her!' I thought, 'she reminds me of myself...', and on an impulse I entered the classroom and introduced myself. She looked up as if I had woken her from a dream; she was beautiful, like a Botticelli, and she had a charming smile; we connected immediately. This was how I met Lucia, or rather Josepha, which was her name before she came to Subud.

I had never known anyone like her. I was bewitched. Whether she did or didn't come to school, her existence gave my life extra meaning; I felt more real, more alive, even as I knew that I was not in love. Also there was that odd resemblance between us, and though she was beautiful while I was just my ordinary self, we did look alike in those days, so that people kept mistaking us on the street, which was strange considering how different we were in every way. In fact, we were opposites: I inclined towards art and books, which didn't interest her in the least. I was down-to-earth, rational, and painfully self-conscious while she was ephemeral, secretive, intuitive and fully aware of her femininity. But it was I who was the optimist, while she was shrouded in an inexplicable melancholy, like a land in twilight, often talking about death and dying so that I feared for her life, imagining her walking into the sea one day and not coming back.

In school Josepha appeared vague and lost in her own world. And sometimes when Dr. Shmueli, our incomparable principal, addressed her with his good-natured irony, 'sorry to interrupt your meditations, but would you help us...' she seemed to come back from far away and hesitate about her answer with an enigmatic smile. Most teachers left her alone, but Mrs. Kathe Jacob, the Dalcroze teacher, recognized her talent and made her demonstrate it in her class. On those occasions Josepha would shine, surprising everyone with her energy and musical aplomb. After all she was a seasoned musician, member of the celebrated Shfeya Mandolin Orchestra, where she played guitar, mandolin, and bass mandolin. There was a steely confidence behind that gentle smile!

I had tried living in Tel-Aviv, but hated it, and chose, instead, to commute home. I liked the lengthy bus rides in the evenings, this time in between when undisturbed I could think and dream freely. But Josepha found herself a picturesque little shack on the beach. It was such a romantic image, this lonely, beautiful girl in her little house with the sea at her doorstep, with the incessant sound of the waves, and the ubiquitous golden sand on her mat covered floor.

The truth was, however, that away from the college and our friendship she led a parallel life of which I knew little. She had many other friends and was as at home in the bohemian circles in the cafés on Dizengof St. as she was with the drifters on the beach. Periodically she needed me for my strength and I needed her for her wings – but we didn't infringe on each other's life. Something else was at work; perhaps it was that 'magic' that drew me to her, or this odd feeling of kinship, as if she was my sister. Whatever it was, it wasn't a regular friendship – it had a lot of space. Even so there was always present this imperceptible undercurrent that nourished and sustained it, that did not let us pull apart and lose touch, until her untimely death twenty years later.

I believe that the following incident happened in the first year, when I was still entirely under her spell.

N. was the VIP of our class. He was the oldest student and had already distinguished himself with a hit song that had made him a household name. And though not prepossessing – chubby, with thinning blond hair, pale blue eyes and a sallow, pockmarked face – he expected and was given due respect. I, however, ignored him. Needless to say, he reciprocated in kind.

I was alone that day when I saw him cross the floor, heading towards my desk. Was he coming to offer an olive branch? Apparently not, for he didn't smile and, towering over me, avoiding my eyes, he declared that he had come as an emissary, and that he was acting on behalf of the whole class.

'Nonsense', I thought, 'this is a plot between you and that busybody girl at the front desk, who's watching us with hawk-eyes as you speak'.

His manner was formal and impersonal; 'I have come to inform you that we are all very concerned about your friendship with Josepha; we believe you are in great danger!'

Incredulous, I nevertheless didn't interrupt him. Instead, I lowered my eyes, fixing them on the diamond pattern of his knitted vest and keeping a straight face let him continue.

'You are a decent girl, but you are from the country and do not know the ways of the city. Therefore we thought to warn you that your association with Josepha does not become you and that it will damage your good name.' He paused.

It was getting stranger by the minute; truly life was imitating art. But I didn't raise my eyes and didn't say a word. This unnerved him a little and, sensing the absurdity of the scene, he softened his voice, becoming more personal. 'Believe me, I know! She is bad news – you can ask anybody in town...' and with one last attempt at credibility he concluded, 'therefore we all advise you, for your own good, to drop this friendship!'

I laughed silently at how this self-important man got caught in such a ridiculous situation; no doubt it was a classic case of sour grapes. But at that moment my main concern was how to finish the scene. For I couldn't help imagining us on stage, in a play, where I had to deliver a fitting punch line – a task for which I felt woefully ill equipped. Thus I only thanked him drily, and told him I could take care of myself, and go mind his own business…

He turned away stiffly, tossing his last words over his shoulder. 'Don't say I didn't warn you!'

For those who may wonder what happened next, I must add that there is no follow up. There was never any trace of malicious gossip, or any interference from the class, who couldn't have cared less; in fact there was nothing. And this is how I perceived the episode from the beginning; as something too much out of the ordinary to have anything to do with this man, his envy, and his frustrated love life. For right away the episode assumed in my mind a gigantic question mark. What was this really all about? Something else was at work here, and instinctively I knew that whatever it was, it would reverberate far into the future. As if I was given a prompting: 'Pay attention, this friendship is important, do not take it lightly.'

The Wayward Years

Soon after graduating from the Music Teachers' College, in the fall of 1961, I left Israel for England. My alleged purpose was to continue there the study of Dalcroze Eurhythmics (a progressive method that employs movement to teach the elements of music). My real purpose however was to put off, for as long as possible, the looming prospect of a life as music teacher. There was also another, lesser reason for my going to London: I had to see my ex boyfriend for one last time; there lingered some unresolved issues that needed to be cleared up. None of it I told my mother or Dr. Shmueli (who had given me a letter of recommendation); and to those who wondered why I was going to England when the Dalcroze centre was in Switzerland, I answered only with a smile and a shrug.

As for Josepha, who from here on I will call by her Subud name, Lucia, she had no freedom to choose. My butterfly friend was caught in an iron mesh; she had to enlist in the army – the thing she had dreaded most.

In London the unfinished affair ended, to everyone's satisfaction, without tears or heartache, but the Dalcroze course was a disappointment. The London college was in the process of phasing the program out altogether, a fact they had neglected to inform the handful of students who had signed up for it. We had no say in the matter and had to recourse to private lessons (that none of us could afford). There was another problem, which I had chosen to ignore until then. Dalcroze requires fluency on the piano. I had taken lessons for the last three years, but wasn't good enough and, to make matters worse, had injured my hands doing too much too soon. In short, the odds were heaping up against this venture, and I dropped out at Christmas.

41

Meanwhile Lucia's army experience turned into a nightmare. She wrote that things were becoming so bizarre she feared of losing her sanity for real. At last someone was found who was able and willing to help, and she was released shortly after. She moved to Jerusalem where she was offered a position with the Jerusalem Radio Orchestra to play the double bass. She wrote there were no problems since it was similar to the bass mandolin; she had only to master the use of the bow.

On the boat on the way to England, I befriended a girl, Michal, an art student, with whom I ended sharing an apartment. Michal was a strong and grounded person with clear ideas of where she was heading and little patience for strugglers like myself; and though her brusque, no-nonsense way was sometimes disconcerting, she was a loyal and trustworthy friend, and I don't know how I would have survived that year without her friendship.

I had also family in London, Lotte and Erwin Saenger, a childless couple who had graciously taken me under their wing. They regularly invited me for dinners, introduced me to their friends and took me along on their weekend outings to the countryside. This was my introduction to bucolic England. I remember lovely picnics and long leisurely walks through ripening fields, over stiles and under magnificent, ancient beech trees. Then it was back to the seething metropolis, where to all appearances I was adrift at sea, a foreigner, living on the fringe of society, doing odd manual jobs, with nary a thought for the morrow. To be away from Israel where everyone knew everybody else, not having to account for my actions, to be swallowed by anonymity, gave me an indescribable sense of freedom. How odd then to be standing in one of London's busiest intersection and behold strolling towards me Messrs. Menahem Mendelson and Shlomo Stein from Beit-Yitzhak!

There was a piano in the first room I rented, but my landlady took exception to my practicing (though I did pay extra for the privilege), and would knock violently on the ceiling whenever I did. Thus one day, keenly missing an instrument of my own, and a quiet one at that, driven blindly, like a sheep by a snapping dog, passing a guitar shop, I entered it on an impulse.

I didn't know the first thing about guitars and wandered about the shop feeling foolish, yet hoping to intuit the one that 'waited' to be mine; they all looked and sounded the same. At last I emerged with a blond guitar, a black guitar case, a tuning fork, a beginner's book, and a new purpose: I was going to teach myself the classical guitar!

The idea wasn't altogether new. The seed had been planted three years earlier on the day I visited Lucia in her little house on the beach in Tel-Aviv. Her guitar was an important accessory in that romantic setting. There it stood in the corner, glowing warmly. It was my first encounter with a guitar. 'May I try?' I asked shyly.

'Go ahead,' she said. But my innate ability to doodle on instruments failed me here miserably; the wide finger board, the frets, the six strings and their tuning threw me off, and embarrassed I said, 'Would you play something for me?' And that was another awkward moment; she became evasive. I had transgressed an implicit agreement regarding the limits of our friendship. All the same she played a short piece by Carulli and I was captivated; I didn't know the guitar could sound that lovely. There and then I vowed: I too shall learn to play it one day! That was the first time I permitted myself to have an attainable dream.

To begin with it was a low-key affair. I realized that I wouldn't go far without help. My first lesson proper was back in Israel, and then, within that first hour, my teacher, Mr. Bakish – an outstanding guitarist – transformed me from a bumbling beginner to an obsessive guitar lover with the lofty goal to be able to play Bach on the guitar.

I was back in August of 1962, and took a part time teaching job in a town near Hadera, halfway between Netanya and Haifa. As I didn't want to live in Beit-Yitzhak I moved to Haifa, which I hoped to make my new home.

Haifa is a charming city with its large bay and bustling harbour; with the rugged beauty of Mount Carmel, and the ubiquitous golden cupola of the Bahai Temple. I found on the Carmel a room with a view, and was slowly learning the ways of the city. Even so, I couldn't shake off the feeling that I wasn't welcome, that Halfa was not my city. And since it was too costly and too far, I returned, defeated, to Beit-Yitzhak.

Lucia, on the other hand, was lucky. She had been invited to join the orchestra on its concert tour in Europe, and when in London she jumped ship. It had always been her dream to live elsewhere, away from Israel. Now, within a year, her dream materialized. London would become her home for the rest of her life.

My life at that point had reached an all-time low. I hated being back in Beit-Yitzhak and hated my work, which was hell. All my innate optimism didn't help me there. For what could one expect to accomplish with large classes of 45 unruly children in weekly one-hour music classes? Then again my status as music teacher was the lowest in school. I was regarded as a kind of appendage-entertainer whose sole justification was to give the real teachers their well-deserved break. Needless to say, the classroom dynamics were intolerable. My few success stories: mandolin and recorder clubs, a middling choir, my winning over one or two classes, could not weigh against the general feeling of frustration, waste and complete uselessness. I had no illusions; to stand in front of a class was not one of my strong points. In retrospect I believe I wouldn't have lasted even that one year if I hadn't got myself embroiled in an obsessive love affair, an affair to end all love affairs. Thus, by divine irony, too engrossed in one hopeless situation, my mind was taken off the bleakness of the other. Mercifully the affair ended in the spring; but when, after finally gaining the support of the principal and the respect of a few teachers, I was transferred to a new school, to start the battle all over again, I balked and resigned two months into the school year.

My mother was beside herself: all that wasted time and money! And what would become of me? She insisted I consult a psychologist. Two sessions and an exorbitant fee sufficed that learned man to advise me that, 'you can do most anything...provided you want to do it.' Good news indeed...

After considering other options: I got accepted to the school for social workers, and had passed entry exams to study psychology – I took instead a secretarial course, hung out on the beach, and come April, packed my bags and returned to London.

My beacon, again, was a young man, a German art student by the name of Norbert. (It didn't last but more about him later.) And like the previous year, London embraced me into its blessed anonymity. Everything was as it had been before; my relatives were as hospitable as ever and if they worried about me they didn't show it. Michal had gone to Paris but Lucia was there and there were many other friends. Most were foreigners, from Israel, Canada, Germany, and Finland. Some claimed to be studying, others, like me, were treading water and biding their time. It should have been a depressing existence, having little money, being nobody, achieving nothing. But we were young, we didn't do drugs and there was always the vague notion that if things became too tough we'd go home. I got back my weekend job in the British Museum cafeteria; I worked as teacher-assistant in a Montessori school; I cleaned homes and gave some Hebrew lessons. Also I went regularly to chamber music concerts at Wigmore Hall, went to the Proms at the Albert Hall, frequented galleries and museums, studied English and French (to keep my student visa) and continued to improve my guitar skills. I didn't waste my time entirely.

I had an uncle in Birmingham, my father's younger brother. The relationship between our families was strained. It had been said that Uncle Walter didn't help my father come to England when he desperately tried to leave Germany. My aunt, however, urged me to visit him regardless. Uncle Walter waited for me on the train platform and was overcome by emotion; he would have recognized me anywhere, he said, I looked so much like Ernst. And in the taxi, reeking of cigars, tears rolling down his fat cheeks, he told me how he suffered years of remorse; that he had paid for his mistake with his sickness; but how could he have known the terrible outcome of the war? 'So it was true,' I thought, and pitied him, but didn't like him. I liked his wife though; she was intelligent, down to earth, with a healthy sense of humour. Lily was purportedly the bad dragon behind the sorry affair. Maybe she was; times were tough then, for the Jews in England too; though I suspected that the root of the problem lay in that timeless sibling rivalry; Walter was the second child, the one who had been 'left out' – it had always been about Ernst and Grete. Had he really wanted to help his brother, Lily would not have stood in his way.

Our second meeting was at the cafeteria of the British Museum. He surprised me; I had told him I worked there, but didn't elaborate. The old snob was aghast: the daughter of Ernst Pinner working at such a lowly job, dressed in that hideous yellow plastic uniform! He stood among the tables I was clearing, trembling with indignation. Then, reaching into his overcoat pocket, he took out his wallet and handed me a few bank notes. I was mortified but also practical: twenty five pounds was a good sum of money in those days, enough to buy a winter supply of coal – Norbert and I wouldn't need to rely on that ridiculous metered gas heater. But that was the last time I saw Uncle Walter.

I left Norbert in early March. Already I had a few guitar students and discovered that I had much to offer. That was when the fog began to lift, when everything was coming into focus, and all the loose ends were converging to one point. I knew exactly what I wanted to do. It was time to go home.

I arrived back in Israel in the late summer of 1965 and promptly moved to Jerusalem. With the generous help of the guitar society there (with Lucia's letter of introduction), I was on my way to establishing myself as a guitar teacher. And within two years I was offered a full-time position at the conservatory of the Rubin Academy.

Sometimes I think how fortunate I had been to fall in love with the guitar. The classical guitar was a relatively new instrument in the sixties, the 'new kid on the block'. Everybody wanted to play it but there were few teachers and few standards. The field was wide open so that someone like me, with only four years of experience, could get a position in a respected music institution and have as many students as I could handle. I was moving with the vanguard, riding on the crest of a wave; it was exciting and inspiring – and I made a good living to boot.

An unimaginable peace descended on me – the sky was the limit.

The Heart

May 1967. Israel was on high alert; the neighbouring Arab states had been amassing their armies along its borders and Gamal Abdul Nasser was rattling his sabres, threatening to wipe Israel off the face of the earth. War was imminent. All the reservists had been called back to the army and the streets were eerily deserted. One stocked up on food and water; windows were taped and prepared for blackout; air raid shelters were fortified with sandbags; there were long line-ups to donate blood; and everyone was glued to the radio; a long and bloody war was expected with untold casualties.

Restless and alone in my apartment I phoned my mother to see how she was doing. Her voice sounded tense. She said that this time she was really frightened.

'Why should you be frightened? Here, in Jerusalem, we have good reasons, but in Beit-Yitzhak? Nothing ever happens there...'

'This is no time for jokes! The Arabs will push us into the sea!'

'Nonsense;'

'It is not! Don't you see? Beit-Yitzhak is on the narrowest stretch of land between the Jordanians and the sea; they will concentrate their attack here and break up the country in the middle.'

I never heard her talk that way; she was not her usual self. Thus on the following morning I travelled to Beit-Yitzhak; she should not be alone over the weekend.

I arrived at noon. She too had just returned from seeing her doctor in Netanya. Lately she had complained of chest pains. The doctor had given her a routine ECG and reassured her that everything was normal. We sat for a while in her living room and talked. I asked if anything had happened to get her into such a nervous state – it was so unlike her.

'My life is too easy now,' she answered bitterly, 'I don't have enough troubles anymore.' (She was retired and living on a comfortable pension from Germany.)

Ignoring her barb I said pleasantly, 'So why don't you do something creative, now that you have more time? Surely for someone of your calibre, looking after chickens and dogs is not enough.'

I was not in the habit of giving my mother advice, but I was brimming with good will and secretly hoped that now that I was settled, and in these stressful times, there would be a change in our relationship, for the better. 'You could write another book' (she had done a translation of the Polish poet Adam Mitskevich into German), 'or perhaps an autobiography?'

But she brushed me off, 'I can't do that anymore, it is all done with; I have nothing to say.' And she got up abruptly and left the room.

At lunch, trying to navigate the conversation into neutral waters, I told her of a volunteer job the guitar society had undertaken, in which we took turns teaching a convict. The man had gained notoriety for a robbery that ended in bloodshed. I told her of his harrowing childhood during World War II, and how, after many years, the widow of his victim, a remarkable Christian woman, in seeking mutual healing, was helping him to rehabilitate. That thanks to her lobbying he was permitted a musical instrument and granted lessons. I told her of his significant musical talent, and how the music was giving him real hope for a new life. (And indeed, within a year he would get married – I was at his wedding – and would be paroled shortly after.)

But my mother only commented drily, 'Don't fall in love with him too...' I dodged her arrow but lost heart: nothing has changed and it never will. And I didn't tell her how much this man resembled my father or that whenever I visited the prison I would think: 'there but for the grace of God, go I...'

In this spirit we finished lunch and she retired to her siesta.

Half an hour later she stumbled into the bathroom violently sick, and collapsed on the floor.

Frightened, I called the local doctor who instructed me to call an ambulance. And etched on my memory is the following scene. It is half-past two in the afternoon under a blazing sun. The ambulance is parked on the path in front of the house. The doctor, a small prim man, stands by, watching. And as the paramedics lift the stretcher into the ambulance, he addresses my mother coolly, with a slight formal bow; 'Well, Mrs. Pinner, it's time to bid you farewell, I doubt we shall ever meet again...'

The nearest hospital was 30 km away, and the ride, on a Friday afternoon, on a congested two-lane road, lasted an eternity. My mother was fighting for her life, gasping and begging for air, but the ambulance was not equipped with oxygen.

'Why didn't the doctor order oxygen?' grumbled the frustrated paramedic, looking at me accusingly. Was I being blamed? I sat beside her utterly helpless. She was alive when they wheeled her into the Emergency, but some minutes later, when they let me in, she was gone.

I stood by her, numb and empty. After the terrible struggle in the ambulance, she looked indescribably serene. How strange, there she was, this strong woman whose personality was so irreconcilable with mine, yet now she wasn't there anymore; there remained only an absolute silence. This body was merely a thing, unconnected to her or anything else.

I don't remember much of what followed: the formalities, the funeral. But I remember the shock I was in; watching myself as if from a very great distance, like through inverted binoculars. Death was a palpable presence, right at my shoulder; and I stared into its black void paralyzed – I might have been dead myself. And on the periphery of my awareness pulsated one dreadful thought: how do I mourn my mother, the woman I couldn't love, who was my greatest obstacle, whom I wanted out of my life?

But I was never left alone. The people of Beit-Yitzhak rallied around me. There was a constant stream of visitors; people I hardly knew and had never spoken to. They brought food and sat with me, talking about their friendship with my mother and what it meant to them, and everything was so real, so essential. These good people didn't let me gaze into the abyss and I was deeply indebted to them.

All too soon, however, before the *shiv'a* was over, I had to return to Jerusalem. It was the last day of the month and I had to sign papers to close the deal on the apartment I had just purchased (with the help of my mother). I travelled in a daze, my heart a desert, my mind a blank; the world around me surreal; the blaring news, the tension, the nervous jostling at the bus station; the pushing and shoving. I did what I had to do and headed back.

The bus pulled out of the city, climbing towards the Arab village of Abu-Gosh. The evening sky was a clear blue, and one white cloud, in the shape of an angel with outstretched wings, hovered above the summit.

'So now you are seeing angels in the sky', said a little ironic voice in my head, 'next you'll believe in God and in miracles!' But I felt strangely comforted, as if a healing hand touched my heart, and this too was a novelty and a marvel.

On June 5th when the hostilities began, I was back in Jerusalem, and staying at a friend's house. We sat in the fortified basement and kept vigil through the night, listening to the radio, hearing the gunfire and shelling in the outskirts of the city, and waiting nervously for the air attack that never came. In the morning we heard the news of the surprise victory of our Air Force. It was the beginning of the Six-Day War.

In the weeks to come, as I went through my mother's effects, I found among her papers an unfinished, typed letter to a Brunnerianer friend. In it she wrote that she couldn't anymore find answers in philosophy, that she got more pleasure out of simple tasks, such as looking after the chickens. That she preferred the company of her dogs to the pretentiousness of the Brunner associates and that she had very little else; she didn't even have the love of her daughter...

A Lame Cat

The cat came into my life in September of 1967, two months after the man did. The cat, as superstition has it, was an omen. Only it took me three years to see it for what it was. In any case the man and the cat are just bookends. This is the story about how I finally made it to Subud.

I moved to my new apartment on the first of September, and feeling magnanimous and wanting to share my new well being with the world, I invited two stray individuals into my home, a man and a cat – respectively.

The man, Jonathan, was an American hippie with a mass of red hair, a guitar, and no fixed address. He was a charming, pleasing fellow, easy-going, intelligent, in no hurry to get anywhere; the perfect houseguest. The kitten, a calico, I rescued from some torturing little boys.

'It's supposed to fall on its feet,' they shouted flinging it down the stairs.

Injured, dragging its hind legs, it would never jump or run, or, as a matter of fact, be graceful, as cats are supposed to be.

So began my *ménage à trois*. Everybody appeared to be thriving. Jonathan employed his time sleeping, playing the guitar and being agreeable. The cat grew fat, had kittens periodically, and generally was finicky and bad-tempered. And I, I was perfectly content to play Family and House. My life seemed to lack for nothing. Ah, yes…there was the little question of marriage: the man was not eager to commit himself; but it didn't darken the rosy glow of my days; there was plenty of time and I put the question out of my mind. For the present I was happy.

And that, apparently, was the prerequisite that got me on to the next level. It all began with a faint uneasiness; the picture was too pretty. 'So at last you are happy,' spoke a little voice in my head, 'you've found your vocation; you make a good living; you have your very own home; and even your love life is quite perfect, well, almost; is that what you wanted for your life, a plateau stretching to the horizon? Aren't you missing something?'

About that time Lucia and her husband, Henry, came to visit her family in Tel-Aviv. They had some playing engagements in Jerusalem and whenever they came up, they stayed at my place. It was then that I noticed something different about them. I had no words to define it; clearly they loved and respected each other, yet they gave each other a lot of space. One sensed a peculiar lightness and tranquillity in their presence.

And then, it was on their last visit, I experienced a *seeing event*, a kind of x-ray vision extraordinaire. It resembled that first time I saw Lucia: through a doorway that acted as a frame to isolate her image from her immediate surroundings. This time I was by the phone in the hall watching her standing in the kitchen talking to someone, and the effect was the reverse. While in college it had been an experience of recognition, now it was of alienation. She had become a stranger; not the butterfly girl I had known, but a grounded woman with a formidable presence. And I could 'see' a vibrating glow, like a charged silver wire that traversed her from top to bottom, connecting her to an invisible higher power. 'This must be Subud!' I thought, and in that split second I envied her and wanted it too.

The vision was over and Lucia was back to her familiar self. But I became shy; for unlike the previous year, when she had talked of nothing else but Subud, this time she and Henry didn't mention Subud even once. Nor did I ask. Words had become absurdly inadequate.

On the day of their departure, slightly embarrassed, I asked her for a Subud contact; just in case. She gave me two numbers: that of the most famous folk singer in Israel, Helena Hendel, and of a well-known radio personality, Hedva Sold. Here was a deterrent! You do not simply ring up famous people. I would have to prepare myself. There was also another 'small' matter to iron out before I made any contact. I had better be clear where I stood on the question of God. Whatever the connection of Subud to God, I didn't want to be unprepared for my first interview.

When we were kids, invariably somebody would stop the game we were at, and ask, 'do you believe in God?' A pause, what an awkward question; one would shrug one's shoulders.

'I don't know – do you?'

'I think I do…I don't know…' We'd continue the hopscotch.

I had not given the question any further thought. I grew up in an entirely secular environment. God had no place in my life, notwithstanding the heavy diet of TANACH studies (the Hebrew Bible) in school; though under the influence of my parents' philosophy I picked up a vague notion that there was one *Elohim*, that His essence resided in all of creation, and that all religions were different roads leading to Him. It made perfect sense and solved my problem with religion: none had the claim to ascendancy; it also didn't put me under any obligation. But did I believe? As I felt I ought to make up my mind, I decided I did, rather than not. It was the best I could do for the present.

A couple of months passed before I mustered the courage to phone Hedva Sold and then, on the way to my first interview I lost an earring – I was not in the habit of losing earrings – was this a sign? The meeting itself was rather awkward. Two ladies, 'helpers', were present, Hedva Sold (who would later change her name to Vardina) and Michal Sadan. But it was less about giving information, which they seemed reluctant to do, and more about measuring each other. I studied them, looking for signs of 'spirituality', while they eyed me guardedly, trying to figure me out. As I had done my homework and had read carefully the printed material I had on hand, and as I understood that Subud was all about an 'exercise' called the *latihan*, which cannot be described but has to be experienced, and as they offered no further explanations, it didn't make sense to ask questions. I left the interview none the wiser, but as I had made up my mind to join, there was nothing to do but wait the three months of probation, though why it was necessary I didn't understand. Hadn't I said I was committed – why wait?

Two weeks later the helpers met with me again to discuss an urgent matter. They had reviewed my situation and realized they had neglected to warn me that, since I was not married, if I joined Subud and consequently experienced personal changes, it might affect my relationship with Jonathan and may even lead to separation. Therefore I should consider my decision carefully; was I still interested? I was amused, not only because of, what I perceived, their prudish notions, but also because I could not see what one had to do with the other. But I answered gravely, surprising even myself, 'whatever will be, will be. If it is God's will, so be it.' The helpers exchanged meaningful looks; I must have said something very profound.

The 'opening' was due on April and we agreed that when the time arrived I would call to set the date. April came and went, May was gone, the summer melted into fall, and I didn't call. To begin with I had final exams (I had been taking additional music courses at the Rubin Academy) and couldn't afford to be distracted; then in the summer everyone was gone; and in the fall life pulled me in other directions so that I forgot – in short, I reneged on my commitment.

In the fall Jonathan had a gig playing in the Khan Theatre, in the mediaeval Singspiel 'Everyman', and there in the audience one evening, I saw Vardina. How embarrassing: I had made a fool of myself having put on such a show... how could I face her now? And so another month went by before I dared contact Subud again.

Now I would have to wait another two months, they said, and to prove my sincerity would have to attend group meetings once a week, to 'sit outside' during latihan. I felt like a child who was being reprimanded, but they apologized; being a young group, they acted upon the counsel of the helpers from the older Subud group in Wolfsburg, Germany.

Latihans were held in a beautiful old house that belonged to the artist Ruth Bamberger. After being introduced to a dozen or so people, I was left alone in the kitchen while the men and women retired to their separate rooms. For a while all was quiet. A cup of tea in front of me I waited nervously, my ears straining, the silence in the house ringing extra loud. Then it began: a sigh, a groan, soft singing that suddenly erupted into shouting, stomping and clapping; calling the names of God, and more singing – quite a cacophony. After a while I relaxed, nothing else seemed to happen and I lost interest. Abruptly the silence returned. The doors opened and people came out, crowding the kitchen. I watched for some aftermath telltale signs but everyone looked disappointingly normal. There were more introductions and small talk and we went home.

My opening was scheduled for a Saturday. The following happened the evening before. I was alone in the apartment doing some ironing, a mindless job, when suddenly a thought raced through my head in flashing billboard letters: '**Jonathan is cheating on you, and has been doing so for the last six months. You are a naïve and pathetic fool!**' I froze, iron in hand, as one after another all the furtive details of the affair came together, to make a perfect case. But of course! – How could I have been so blind?

I confronted him as he entered the apartment. He admitted to everything, and I ordered him to pack his bags and 'leave, now!' Like in the movies: secretly, in a perverse way, I was enjoying myself.

'But she cannot take me in tonight; can't you wait till the morning?'

He was so charmingly helpless. I kept to my drama queen script. Now came the moment to throw a tantrum. A few flying objects, a broken plate. And an hour later I was alone in my living room, trembling. We had been together nearly three years.

On the following day I didn't tell anyone what had happened. Visitors had arrived from Tel-Aviv, but amidst all the congratulations I felt numb, like the survivor of a car crash. All I wanted was to get on with it. I was ushered into the room sans shoes and jewellery. The ladies, in long dresses, stood in a circle, waiting quietly. As Michal Sadan, led me to the centre, I became alarmed: was this going to be an embarrassing, arcane initiation? But no; she produced a small booklet and in a matter of fact voice proceeded to read a short statement. I was asked to confirm my belief in God or, if I preferred, in a Universal Power, and advised to close my eyes, pay no attention to anyone around me, and follow whatever arose from within with an attitude of patience, surrender, and trust. Then she said, 'Begin', and the by now familiar din started – only I was in its midst. Overwhelmed, I remembered to relax and wait. Next I was sobbing violently. My brain kept a detached commentary: 'Of course, what do you expect – you have good reasons to cry; this is not the latihan!' But the sobbing was deep and releasing and seemed to have nothing to do with yesterday's anger; what happened yesterday had lost all its importance. Soon I was singing at the top of my voice, feeling a surge of happiness I didn't know existed, and then my legs buckled underneath me and I fell on my knees, my forehead touching the floor, in an attitude of prayer. Well! I had never prayed before, nor been on my knees in supplication! If I doubted my crying, this convinced me. This was the latihan. 'Finish!' said a voice, and it was over.

A small party had been arranged to welcome me as a new sister, but I needed solitude and begging their forgiveness, went out into the night to catch my bus. I was therefore not too pleased to see at the bus stop one of the women with whom I had just done latihan. Some small talk was expected after all.

'Well…what do you think?' she asked.

'What do you mean?' I tried to conceal my irritation.

She tossed her head in the direction of the open field, the dark silhouettes of the olive trees, the distant lights of the city; the world.

'I mean about this whole Subud thing…'

There was something infuriating in her voice; I could sense that she was one of those who all their lives sit teetering on a fence, and I had no wish to talk. With an effort at civility I asked, 'how long have you been in Subud?'

'Six months'

'And what do you think?'

'I don't know…' her plaintive, soft voice trailed off. 'I am not sure it is the thing for me…'

She looked at me as if she expected support or sympathy. I gave her none. 'Funny,' I thought, 'here I am, directly after the most momentous experience of my life, and of all people I am in the company of a doubter.'

'I am sure,' I said and reiterated, 'I am very sure.'

Realizing she had stepped out of bounds she assumed a nonchalant tone.

'Then I am glad for you, I wish you luck.'

'I wish you luck too,' I thought as I got off the bus.

Approaching my apartment building, I noticed a dark shape lying on the ground; was it a dead cat? Getting nearer I found out that indeed it was; and it was mine! My poor, lame cat had been hit by a car. She was too awkward and too slow to dodge it.

How Does A Mexican Woman Laugh?

My life now revolved around the latihan and my new Subud family. I floated through the days in a state of euphoria, my feet barely touching the ground. An associate who didn't know what had happened noted, 'you are taking the break-up with J. wonderfully! You are practically glowing; do you have somebody else in your life?'

But Lucia in a letter cautioned that this was only a Subud honeymoon; that Subud was not an easy path and that it would become difficult by and by.

Of all my friends and family members, only one trusted my word implicitly and joined Subud three months after I did. It was peculiar: here I was brimming with enthusiasm, broadcasting from the roof tops the best news ever. 'Hey everybody, God really IS! You don't have to *believe* in him, come to Subud and witness for yourself His power through the latihan!' But nobody cared and within a short time I lost, one by one, most of my friends. I had become an insufferable zealot.

About that time I received a letter from Mr. Rosenzweig, a member of the Constantin Brunner Society. He had never written me before and I was somewhat surprised. He wrote that he had learned about my joining Subud from my brother Stephan. That after careful reading he became quite alarmed and, as a friend of my mother's, felt it was his duty to warn me against this Subud, before it was too late. Evidently Subud was one of those bizarre cults you read about these days, and most likely I was being brainwashed and conned; it was simply too good to be true! Didn't I know that Humanity had forever been seeking for this very spiritual experience, and that only a few chosen had received it, like Moses and Jesus, the prophets and the saints? How presumptuous to claim that now it was available to everybody! Above all he feared that I was in great peril of meddling with spiritual matters far beyond my scope, which, in all likelihood, would lead me to insanity.

It was a remarkable letter, since Mr. Rosenzweig seemed to understand what Subud is all about. Only I resented his interfering and his patronizing tone, and send back a rash and impertinent reply, to which he never responded.

In the spring the word went out that Bapak would be visiting Germany in July, and nearly everyone in Subud Israel began making travel plans; but I didn't. That Bapak was the founder of Subud was a given, yet unconsciously I relegated him to the past, like Abraham or King David – a legendary figure hidden in the mist of time – so that he remained an abstraction. And as to his photograph in the latihan room, there was something about it that kept me at bay, that didn't let me see the man beyond the image, or reconcile my experience of the latihan with it. Why was it there anyway? Born under a rebellious sign I abhor adulation. The fact that the latihan works independently of Bapak was of the utmost importance. Therefore the mere notion of going to see him went against the grain for me.

One day a Subud sister from Tel-Aviv inquired, 'are you coming with us to Germany?'

'No.'

'You should test about it you know; to see Bapak is a unique experience. If I were you I would ask the helpers to test with me. You never know, you may get a surprise…' She chuckled knowingly. 'Infuriating busybody,' I thought, but gave her credit for her frankness.

Testing (asking a question and receiving an answer in the latihan, by surrendering the question to God) was still a novelty. I had only one previous encounter, which though impressive, had left me nonplussed. There was no particular reason for this testing session; it was simply out of curiosity. 'Curiosity killed the cat', and I surely got more than I had bargained for!

After establishing that I received 'Yes' and 'No', the helpers suggested two 'harmless' questions: What was my attitude towards myself, and what should it be? And without warning I got hit by a direct missile when, for the first question, I collapsed on the floor in utter despair so that if I could I would have dug a mile-deep hole and buried myself therein, while for the second I stood tall, my arms reaching upwards in prayer. All told an unsettling experience, since as a novice it was bad enough to face this darkness within me, of which I had but an inkling; but then there was the impossible question, what do I do with such 'knowledge'? What was it good for? Where was the bridge that would lead me from this total self-loathing to self-acceptance?

All the same I tested with the helpers about going to see Bapak, and the answer was far beyond a simple affirmative; I felt like a rocket launched into space – this trip was to be one of the most significant events of my life!

Chastised and slightly dazed, I proceeded to make the necessary arrangements. It was too late to join the others; I would have to travel alone.

At this point I had to learn an odd lesson that would be repeated on many other occasions. Travelling for Subud meant 'business' and I was not to mix business with pleasure. For I had no intention to go directly to Germany, but planned to visit Paris first, and then, possibly, also Brittany. From there on things went strangely haywire. First I had a burglary, where nothing in the apartment was disturbed, except that the envelope with the extra (illegal) foreign currency was gone. Then, in Rome, I missed my connection to Paris and was left stranded in the airport in the middle of the night (not recommended for single female travellers), and when I arrived in Paris I fell sick and had to stay in bed for the greater part of the visit; and forget Brittany.

It was like the return of the prodigal son when I reunited with the Israelis and met the friendly members of Subud Hamburg. I had been to Germany twice before. One visit, a business trip to Berlin, was a harmless, uneventful tourist like affair; but on the other – a 24 hour stay-over in Munich, I witnessed in a bizarre succession of events, blatant vestiges of Nazism, anti-Semitism and xenophobia that confirmed my deep dislike for the country. Now I was in Hamburg and in a week's time would follow Bapak to Wolfsburg. But here was an altogether different Germany. The members of Subud Hamburg and Wolfsburg were wonderfully generous, and the guests, who came from all over the world, were literally cocooned in this beautiful bubble of hospitality. It was a true Subud Shangri-La and pure magic.

In Hamburg, I had my first 'Bapak experience'. The eager, almost feverish, preparations for Bapak's visit were at their peak, but I watched the commotion with disbelief; all that fuss ... these lovely people were slightly out of their minds and over the top and, frankly, it was pretty embarrassing.

And so it was that at the hour of Bapak's arrival I stood to the side, determined not to be carried away and to watch everything with detachment and a clear eye. Still I couldn't control the beating of my heart when I saw Bapak, his wife Ibu, and entourage, coming down the red carpet. Little blond boys with baskets walked in front scattering rose-petals, and the people crowding the path stood beaming reverently. I said to myself, 'Relax, see, he is only a man', but then suddenly he wasn't anymore. That old switch in my brain was turned on again, and I saw an almost mythical personality, taller, regal, surrounded by a palpable unseen aura that separated and raised him far above the throng.

Recently I saw an old footage of that event. There remained no trace of the magic. Bapak looks like an elderly Indonesian dignitary in a dark suit, not particularly tall, smiling benevolently. The camera had flattened the event, transforming it into something mundane and insignificant.

But there in the summer of 1970 in Hamburg, as my brain was automatically silenced, the Bapak I saw that first time was not someone I could even call a man. I had of course no need to talk or explain. I just let myself be swept along, like everybody else, by these new sensations of wonder and love.

To my first Bapak-talk, I came armed with pen and paper. Bapak's voice was clear and rich, a pleasure to listen to even if one didn't understand the language. He talked for long stretches of time, which then were followed by translation; and while I stayed focused, writing busily, simultaneously translating into Hebrew, I observed that many people had their eyes closed and were swaying gently, while others appeared fast asleep. Later I was laughed out of town; what was I doing with pen and paper? I was not expected to remember his words. Bapak didn't address the intellect but the inner feeling. I would do better just to be in a quiet state and if I fell asleep it would mean that my brain was not capable as yet to deal with the situation. 'Don't worry; your inner will get what it needs...' I followed the advice dutifully and slept through many a talk.

But the crowning event was my first experience testing with Bapak. It was so momentous I considered it as my second opening. I don't know how many we were, but the floor of the auditorium was packed. I stood beside one of those beautiful, awesome women from Subud Wolfsburg, feeling inexperienced and exposed. (The men, meanwhile, waited their turn in the bleachers.)

Before he began with the testing, Bapak gave a short explanation to the effect that the latihan we are doing enables us to unite our feelings with all humanity; that it is the key that can truly open our hearts to embrace people of every race, religion and nation. This is a sample of the questions we were asked to receive: to show in our movements how a Javanese woman dances? How does a princess walk? How does a peasant? How does an English woman laugh? Et cetera ...

'Embarrassing kindergarten stuff,' I thought, feeling terribly self-conscious while receiving the graceful movements of a Javanese dancer. My running commentary went something like this: 'Am I really receiving or am I just playacting? – American dancing? Ugh, how debasing! – A princess... Is it a fairytale princess or a real one? – A peasant? Ah, but I am a peasant; this is too familiar; these tests do not work for me... An English lady?... Yes! I have lived among them and seen that intimidating smile; it is quite something to be inside it! – How does a Mexican woman laugh? I've no idea! I never met one and have never heard the laughter.'

But at this point my brain finally shut up as a surge of incredible strength shot through me, and standing in a posture of defiance, my legs firmly on the ground, my arms akimbo, I began to laugh. It was an explosive belly laughter that was impossible to fake. Where did this come from, this energy and love of life?

As we left the auditorium I overheard my lovely neighbour mutter under her breath, 'I dread these tests with Bapak when he asks us to receive laughter. It seems I cannot laugh.'

Subud Wolfsburg had organized an outing to the countryside, to 'a typical' German forest – actually a man-made plantation and a far cry from the old forest of the Grimm fairy tales. Yet the moment we stepped onto its eerily thick and soundless needle floor, where nothing seemed to grow, an instantaneous hush fell on the company, as if we had entered a cathedral. And as we traipsed among the pine trees, their trunks bare and tall, standing in orderly rows, like battalions of giants on the march; delighted to discover enormous spotted red and white toadstools, and expecting little people to peek from behind every tree and stone – I began to experience a maddening sensation of déjà vu. But then when we left the forest and walked along its outskirts, where brambles grew, and where occasionally one came across bright green patches of wild blueberries, the déjà vu escalated to an intolerable pitch. 'I know this place; I have been here before!' Only of course I haven't.

Later that day some of us were invited to Viviana Bulow-Hube, the renowned silversmith, for tea. I was early, and upon entering her living room, I saw on the coffee table a book – obviously placed there intentionally. It was an old German children book, a slim volume, exquisitely illustrated – and it took my breath away. For this book used to be my most cherished, most favourite book. And overcome by strange emotions I thought what kind of treachery, what betrayal, had caused it to be so completely eradicated from my memory? Viviana called out something from the kitchen but I was gone, transported to the lost world of my early childhood, re-living a forgotten moment of indescribable sweetness; being tucked into bed, my mother sitting beside me reading from this very book and I lost in its magical and delicate illustrations.

It's the story of two children who are sent to the forest to gather berries. Finding none and not daring to return empty-handed, they fall asleep on the forest floor. That's when the little people come out. They transform the children to their own size and take them, riding on the back of snails, to their secret berry patches. All pitch in to pick the berries, now as large as apples, climbing ladders to pile them into the baskets that are as big as houses. In the morning the children awake to find their baskets brimming with red and blue berries.

This then was the answer to the déjà-vu. Indeed I had been to that forest many times – in my childhood fantasies. But like much else that would happen to me in Subud, this was far more significant than just a pretty anecdote; it was nothing less than the launching of my protracted journey towards the reconciliation with my mother.

I hold in my hand a photograph taken at the airport: Bapak and Ibu and their company sitting in the lounge, children at their feet, and behind a small crowd of people standing close together, watching, their faces expressing gentle love and the sadness of parting.

I am not in the photo since I was standing by the far window, looking out onto the runway. 'For heaven's sake,' I thought, 'won't you give Bapak some air, why crowd him so!' When suddenly my legs began to move of their own accord, and with a sense of inevitability, I approached the little group – it was like an inner command; I could no longer remain sitting on the fence. When I arrived Bapak turned his head in my direction and gave me a look as if to say, ah, so there you are!

With Bapak gone, I began having excruciating pains in my chest so that for a few days I walked about unable to breathe, believing I was going to die.

Years later I had had the fortune to see Bapak again on numerous occasions, but the intensity of that first goodbye was never repeated.

Bapak passed away in the early morning of June 23, 1987, hours after his 86th birthday celebration. When the news reached me, I experienced, like many other Subud members, a great sense of shock and loss, and at the same time a wondrous feeling of serenity. And yet, I could not ignore also the presence of another less noble emotion – a childish disappointment; Bapak had let me down! For I had been recently appointed as international helper, and was looking forward to go to Indonesia, to Cilandak, in July, to attend the World Subud Council meeting, with Bapak present. I had never been there and secretly hoped that Bapak would offer me some council, as he was wont to do sometimes, to help straighten me out a little.

So I watched my heart, that possessive organ, and questioned its tranquillity. When I understood that my heart wasn't grieving because it already had said its final goodbye 17 years earlier! This is what that pain in Wolfsburg was all about. It meant that henceforth I wasn't permitted to cling to Bapak in any shape or form. I loved him and will love him in my soul forever, but from that first heart-piercing goodbye onwards I was required to find my own way, as Bapak had said many times: I had to learn to stand on my own two feet.

What's In a Name?

On the legal form giving a reason for the name change, Subud members in Israel quoted the Jewish philosopher Maimonides, or *Ha'Rambam* (1135-1204): 'A man who truly wishes to repent ought to change his name, leave his city and beseech his Father in heaven for forgiveness.'

I had known of the practice of name change in Subud long before I joined it. It was in all the papers. Nechama Hendel, the folk singer and darling of Israel, had changed hers to Helena, a *gentile* name! And what a hue and cry ensued. Some went so far as to accuse her of betraying her country and her roots. Personally I thought the whole affair way over the top; but after a year in Subud, I too felt the need for change and sent Bapak a request for a new name. How paradoxical, therefore, that at that point I let a stale and old voice latch itself onto my bandwagon.

It was the summer before school and I expected the worst. Everybody in Beit-Yitzhak had heard the story about Fritzi Cohen; how on the first day in class his teacher announced: 'How can you live in the Land of Israel and go to a Hebrew school with a German name like Fritzi! We will give you a Hebrew one. From now on you shall be called Dan.'

I was aware that my name was Christian, and feared a similar fate. Such an exposure was unthinkable and I begged my mother to change it. But I was named Magdalena after a family friend who was still alive; a name change was out of the question. Always resourceful, my mother offered a compromise – Magda. It sounded Hebrew, and I could argue that its origin is Hebrew, after Miriam from the town of *Migdal*, which means a tower. I was disappointed, but as my mother had predicted, I encountered no problems. Still, I didn't like it and in my daydreams I gave myself heroic Hebrew names like Miriam, Michal and Ruth.

Upon receiving from Bapak the letter 'S' I had it all figured out; I was going to kill two birds with one stone. I would get from Bapak my *true* name and it will be Hebrew into the bargain. Thus I had on my list (to send back to Bapak) four lovely Hebrew names beginning with 'S', but the fifth posed a problem. For in latihan I kept receiving the name *Sivana*; I didn't know of such a name, but it felt exceptionally good; the only difficulty was that it implied that I was born in the month of *Sivan*, the Hebrew equivalent for June, which wouldn't do since I was born in *Iyar*. Nevertheless, I added it to the list.

Bapak's reply came: 'The name that is right for Magdalena Pinner is "SILVANA".'

I protested, 'Bapak had made a mistake! *Someone* had made a mistake! This was *not* on my list, and it isn't a *Hebrew* name!'

And so it came to pass that when this beautiful and rare name alighted into my life I welcomed it quibbling...

There is a curious postscript to this story. About that time I had a friend by the name of Sylvain. He was a bit of an oddball, but I liked him for his sensitivity and his quirky sense of humour. He was Catholic and had been contemplating monastery life. His attitude to Subud was ambivalent, to say the least. Once, when I kept rhapsodizing about it (I did so believe that Subud was 'just the thing' for him), he put me sharply in my place: 'You talk as if you had just invented God!' Right, point taken!

That evening he came for dinner, and while he stood in the hall taking off his coat I said cautiously: 'by the way, I got a reply from Indonesia; my new name has arrived...' I paused, 'it is Silvana!'

The coincidence of the names Sylvain and Silvana was quite amusing, like Papageno and Papagena, the comic characters from Mozart's opera 'The Magic Flute'. Would he share the joke? But he stood as if paralyzed, his face turning ashen pale, then hastily he put back on his coat muttering: 'I knew it!' And avoiding my eyes he said, 'I have to go...'

He was gone never to show up again!

The other name-story happened eight years later. By then I had immigrated to Canada, was newly wed, and lived on a farm in southern Ontario. I had just gone through the trauma of a lengthy, drawn-out miscarriage, and was still struggling with bouts of depression.

Wandering aimlessly one afternoon in the bush, blinded by tears, I became aware of a force that had taken hold of my legs and was leading me off the path and into the thicket. Having read the books of Carlos Castaneda I questioned if this was the latihan or something else, but as it felt benign I let myself be led, keeping my eyes on the ground to watch my step. Finally my legs came to a halt and I raised my eyes expecting something out of the ordinary, but there was nothing to see, only a small clearing surrounded by brush. So what was this all about? Why was I led to this spot? Carefully I looked around for a hint. I was standing by a fallen tree trunk that sprawled across the clearing. As I followed it with my eyes, the way one would follow a chalked arrow in a game of clues, I saw it. At the other end of the trunk stood its remaining jugged stump and from its rotting centre sprang a tall sapling, its convoluted root system hugging the mother stump, its branches reaching unhindered for the sun. Behold – a sign!

That year, after the World Congress of 1979 in Toronto, I became pregnant again. When it was time to send for names for the unborn, I hesitated: I had received in latihan that I would have a daughter and that her name would be Ilana. Should I send for a name regardless, or should I trust my receiving? I wanted to do what was right by my unborn. Then one evening I got a long distance call from Toronto, from my friend Darlene: a strange thing had happened to her in latihan, she said, she had a receiving that the child I was carrying was a girl, and that her name was 'something like Elana or Alana; was there such a name?'

Here was the affirmation I needed; I left it at that.

<u>Note</u>: Ilana is a popular Hebrew name. It was first introduced by Israel's national poet Chaim Nachman Bialik. It is the feminine form of the name *Ilan*, which means a tree.

PART THREE
TRUE TALENT

Con Alma

A man is searching under a streetlight.
A passer-by asks: 'Have you lost something?'
'Yes, my money.'
'Where did you lose it?'
'Over there.'
'Then why are you looking here?'
'The light is shining here isn't it? How can I search there in the dark?'
 - A Yiddish Joke

I was told that my search had began early, that already by the age of five I had announced (to the great amusement of the family) that I was not going to live in Beit-Yitzhak for the rest of my life. My teens were the usual fare of giddy discontent and frustration, but in my twenties the search became a fixation; who am I; why am I so different; what is it that I was born to do? With no ready answers, my search led me into one blind alley after another, and despair lurked just around the corner.

Strange how sometimes we remember in vivid details a seemingly insignificant incident. Such a one happened in Paris, in the spring of 1965. My friend, Michal, and I were sitting in Café Select when a man strolled in with that feigned vagueness of a cat on the prowl. He was middle aged, wearing a suit that has seen better days, his sensitive, worn face betraying traces of a dandy; and my antennae went up; uh oh, watch out! Sure enough, sighting us, he made a beeline in our direction and offered to read our palms. We declined his offer. Undaunted, borrowing a chair from a nearby table, he sat down at ours and while we continued our conversation in Hebrew, pretending to ignore him, he commenced to scrutinize us with impudence. He then addressed me in English.

'I have been watching you and I can't make you out. You are a strange girl. Everything about you is a contradiction; your hands are beautiful, they have life (he got me there, I was proud of my hands), but they do not fit your body; and your face is a baby's face (ouch!) – as if you are asleep – and then your eyes, they don't match your face, they belong to someone else…Who are you?'

Of course I wasn't fooled; for all I knew it was his regular sales pitch. Yet there was something uncanny in the way he saw through me. His words touched a raw nerve and I wanted to hear more, but my no-nonsense friend signalled that it was time to shake him off, and we got up and left.

With the advent of the guitar I came close to the belief that my restless quest was over. 'I could do this for the rest of my life', I thought blissfully. And indeed, for a few years I was fulfilled and at peace. But then I went to Spain and had a fling with flamenco. It was the short and intense kind of affair that can easily be construed as a passing infatuation. Yet it spurred a disconcerting 'tectonic' shift that ultimately led me away from the music onto a renewed quest – the search for my true talent.

It was somewhat odd; I had been to most of Western Europe except for Spain and Portugal; but whenever I thought of going I felt I should wait, that visiting Spain would happen in a specific, yet unknown, context.

The summer of 1968 offered just that. I was travelling with Jonathan; we planned to buy a car in Amsterdam and head directly to Spain, stopping only in Paris. We had specific goals; Jonathan to study flamenco, and I to find a good guitar. And though sightseeing was not a priority I stipulated that we'd break our relentless crossing to visit Granada on our way south, and Cordoba, Madrid, and Toledo on the way back. Toledo was important; the painting of Toledo by El Greco, with its greenish light and stormy skies had haunted me since childhood. (Toledo was reduced to a day's excursion, and I didn't find there what I was looking for. El Greco's painting remained aloof, and its magic intact.)

This was, by the way, the summer of the notorious student unrest in Paris, and travelling through that beautiful city it was jarring to see the streets punctuated by ugly concrete barricades, and everywhere the ominous presence of gendarmes. This was also the summer when the free world was stunned by Russia's invasion of liberal Czechoslovakia. We, however, headed south, across the Pyrenees, to Barcelona.

There, in a nightclub, I had my first taste of live flamenco. 'This isn't real flamenco!' hissed Jonathan contemptuously; 'wait till we get to the south...'

Embarrassed, I conceded that it was somewhat sleazy – nonetheless I thought it marvellous!

The Mecca for flamenco aficionados was the town of Moron de la Frontera and thither we drove, stopping nowhere but Granada. During our 5-day stay in Barcelona I visited every guitar shop in the city, but didn't find what I was looking for. It was in Granada in a small shop on a narrow street leading to the Alhambra that I found my guitar. It was love at first sight, and though it had a larger than average fingerboard – made to fit Segovia's huge hands and sausage fingers – it had a soul, and I was bewitched. My hands never 'grew' to fit it comfortably but I remained loyal to it till the end – until a stroke, thirty years later, forced me to give up playing altogether.

Moron de la Frontera had but one attraction; it was the home of the legendary flamenco guitarist Diego del Gastor (1908-1973). His legend was compounded by the fact that Diego refused to be recorded. And though unauthorized tapes were copied and passed from one zealous fan to another, the only way to really grasp his music was to meet him in person.

Moron was a poor, sun-baked, gypsy town. We found lodging in one of the only two pensions – a pleasant but bug-infested place. (The bedbugs preferred the tender skin of my redheaded companion and left me in relative peace.) We took long siestas in the afternoons, hung out in the main café drinking cheap red wine, befriended the stray dogs that roamed the town in packs, and lived flamenco 24 hours a day.

We were lucky; on the day of our arrival there was a major flamenco festival in the vicinity. I thought we were in for a treat, like that nightclub show minus the sleaze, and should have suspected that it would be very different when I noticed that we were, conspicuously, the only non-Spaniards in the crowd. For it was, in fact, a national competition that proceeded with pomp and ceremony, with an endless procession of performers, young and old, all in formal evening attire, with the audience rooting for their favourites. I, however, became increasingly restless; there were no signs of it ending any time soon; the seats were hard; I understood little Spanish and had no idea what was going on. There was hardly any solo guitar playing, and little dancing. The competition was for singers.

I confess to not being a great fan of vocal music and singers in general, but this was totally incomprehensible. What to make of all that wailing, the raspier the voice the better? And what were they shouting/singing about? And why did the crowd OLE` whenever they did? Most disappointing, however, was the performance of the celebrated dancer, the 'Queen of Flamenco'. There she stood on the stage erect and proud, like a queen, wearing an austere white gown, a white flower in her gathered black hair and – for heaven's sake – she was barefoot! No foot tapping?! And forget the castanets! Her dance was dignified and subtle. It was all about grace and restraint. Fair enough; but I was bored out of my wits.

'This is pure classic flamenco dancing!' I was chided, 'you should count yourself lucky to witness this extinct art-form!'

About midnight there came an imperceptible change. Numb with fatigue and tedium, I suddenly began to grasp *what* made the crowd roar. It was odd how this raw, utterly foreign music opened my ears to the existence of an *inner* dimension I had never really been aware of. For this music was not about virtuosity, or the beauty of the voice, or the charisma of the performer, but about integrity! When a passage was delivered from an inner place – so that it felt real, as if chipped off the performer's soul, thus touching the soul of the listener, then the crowd roared their OLE!

It was a true revelation; and deeply moved, filled with the fervour of the newly converted I joined the crowd shouting from the bottom of my heart, OLE!

The concert ended towards morning and, leaving the amphitheatre, I was a changed woman, wide-awake, and smitten.

When Jonathan began his lessons with Diego I tagged along. Flamenco has no written tradition, and as Jonathan didn't trust his memory, I volunteered to write down some of the *falsetas* (passages) Diego demonstrated. But Diego and his friends teased me for days afterwards; what was there to write? It was all about listening, keeping *compas* (rhythm), and playing *con alma* (with the soul). Diego said that Flamenco cannot exist without *duende*, the spirit of flamenco, and lamented that nowadays few had the gift to play from the soul; that the art of flamenco was in decline. He blamed the recording business for corrupting the musicians.

Two nephews studied with him; Augustin, the older, was a true virtuoso; and though currently nursing a thumb injury, the moment his hand healed, he said, he was out of this hole, heading for Barcelona, to seek his fame and fortune. Diego shook his head sadly: he plays very fast, very good, but not with the soul. If he goes north, he will be lost; he will sell his soul to Mammon. The second nephew, Diego junior, was a sensitive musician intent on following in his uncle's footsteps to becoming a true flamenco guitarist: as in having regard for the deeper meaning of the music, complementing the singing and dancing, and aiming at unifying the event.

We were fortunate to be invited to a number of *juergas*, informal flamenco parties, with lots of wine and food and hours of music. Great artists came to those parties, and the more I heard the more I admired the artistry of Diego and his musician friends, and the more I became engrossed in the complexity and the depth of this music.

By the end of our stay I understood just about everything that was being said in Spanish (though I couldn't speak it), and had become familiar with most of the flamenco community. Among them was an American woman who had introduced herself as an 'American Gypsy'. Her son, a talented 19-year-old, studied with Diego and painted inspired Van Gogh landscapes. She was in her forties, with heavily lined blue eyes, masses of wild auburn hair, long skirts and heavy jewellery. I thought she was 'flaky', but then she impressed me one day when she said, 'you don't look at all Jewish, but your eyes give you away, I can see in them all the sorrow of the Jewish people.'

Ah yes; she had touched a hidden chord: being in Spain felt like *déjà vu*, like coming home; as if I had been here in a previous lifetime; maybe in the Golden Age of the Jewish Diaspora under the rule of the Moors, or perhaps I was among those expelled in 1492 by Ferdinand and Isabella...

We had been invited to an informal afternoon party at her home. She lived in a sprawling run-down villa, hidden by a high wall overgrown with bougainvillea. She had nothing but the bare minimum; most of the rooms flanking the inner courtyard were empty, their walls mouldy and cracking. There were present Diego senior and junior, our hostess and her son, Jonathan, and I. Diego got the seat of honour, a dilapidated cane-chair, and everyone else sat on mattresses on the floor. We drank wine out of metal cups and ate watermelon and each took turn playing the guitar.

Suddenly Diego turned to me, 'Now you play something!' I protested that I didn't play flamenco. 'No,' he said 'Play *your* music!' I was at a loss: my music was out of place in the context of flamenco; too light, even frivolous. Bach would have worked, but I didn't trust myself to do him justice; so I chose two pieces from the Italian Renaissance. And as I played for the maestro a little miracle happened. Generally I was a nervous performer, but on this occasion I felt totally relaxed, aware of my playing, and of how the music touched my listeners. The experience was extraordinary, as if a force was playing through me, I only being its channel. 'This must be because of Diego,' I thought, 'he listens with his soul and thus he lifted mine...'

When I began to do the latihan, as it slowly touched and awakened the various aspects of my being, I expected that it would also change and deepen my playing. Instead I hit a snag when I became aware of an inner barrier, like an invisible glass wall, that separated my playing from my inner feeling. I could almost *see* through it, yet couldn't reach beyond. Clearly playing con Alma cannot be willed or taught; it is a Gift and I didn't have it.

This was nothing new since, deep down, I had known it all my life. And indeed it wasn't a sudden crisis, but a slow process of erosion that took months and years. I tried to ignore the stultified feeling, the lessening of my commitment, the increased boredom. But such disappointment doesn't go away and eventually I had to face the truth. The guitar that should have been the gold that was to sustain me for life turned into fools-gold. I was back at square one, right where I began – or thereabouts.

When it became so intolerable that I could barely touch the instrument, I tested with the helpers. Was this general discontent a hint that I should start looking in a different direction? But the guidance was decisive; I should keep to the music and everything that relates to it; it was not the time for change; I should not give in to whims and weaknesses and I should thank the Almighty for this profession which was providing me with a good living. And so I did.

Kaleidoscope

When my daughter was seven I bought her a kaleidoscope for the same reason I gave her a teddy bear on her first birthday; to bring back my own childhood. She didn't care much for either and the kaleidoscope ended up collecting dust on the mantelpiece. I, on the other hand, played with mine often, meditating with longing and frustration on its skittish configurations. So I took the kaleidoscope apart to get to the bottom of it, and was left with a miserable heap of coloured glass and a piece of mirror.

And this is what I am doing presently; pulling my childhood apart, searching for signs of an early artistic potential and looking for answers to why it was ignored. But the signs are faint and unreliable. In all likelihood I will end up with a similar miserable heap of facts.

Sitting at the edge of the bed after a heavy, sleepless night, a clear thought hits my brain, like a splash of cold water.

'This was the biggest botch-up of your life but there's no one to blame – though if you wish, you could blame the school system!'

So my mother and the rest of the family are off the hook; what a relief!

Later, as I try to regroup, a limpid image of red tulips rises before my eyes – the graceful, wild tulip of my childhood. The flower came up every spring and could be found everywhere in Beit-Yitzhak; but then it fell victim to cultivation, indifference, and the greed of marauding children – and became extinct.

I get the drift. I needn't try so hard to prove my 'precocity', since, like the wild tulip it was there, for all to see. Yet also like it, having to contend with unfavourable conditions, my talent had little chance to survive.

I thought it best to start with Hanania, though there existed already before his arrival a small, faded art portfolio from kindergarten, which I treasured for years. But I shall leave that one alone. Hanania's arrival had an enormous impact on my life. Here was this previously unknown big brother, come home from the war. He was an artist and a mystery. He was handsome and gentle, and I never took him for granted – he was more like an uncle than a brother. There was something foreign about him: a lingering smell of army uniform, a whiff of faraway places. I remember how inept he looked when helping around the house or on the farm, and how he would change – becoming steely and focused – when, sitting slightly apart from the family, watching us intently, he would begin to sketch. Or how, seemingly preoccupied, he would roll between his fingers cigarette silver paper, moulding it into miraculous miniature figurines; or his infinite patience when he copied drawings by Rembrandt and Durer. The family joked that Hanania lacked for nothing if he had in his shirt pocket a sketchbook, pencils, and a toothbrush. Intense and dreamy, philosophical and impractical – what were my parents thinking when they sent him to learn the trade of house painting?

It was after Hanania had left for Ein-Gev that I began to draw from life – furtively, so as not to be accused of being a copy cat – sketching and doodling on loose bits of paper or in the margins of my school books. I was proud when I caught a good likeness but my heart wasn't in it; I knew I could never draw as well as Hanania – I didn't even know how to draw a horse!

There were no art classes in school. Art was considered an excessive and frivolous subject. Coloured pencils were employed only for colouring maps in Geography – which is how I got my good mark in that subject. Girls were taught knitting, sewing and embroidery and the boys did woodwork and metalwork.

But then, inexplicably, for one year only – in grade six – we received a trial art class. Albeit taught by the shop teacher – a carpenter. My initial excitement fizzled quickly away when we were assigned to design, respectively, a belt, a Rosh Hashanah greeting card, a Hanukkah menorah, and a tablecloth for the Shabbat. However, there were two memorable exceptions. The first was to fill a page with random scribble, and colour in the in-between spaces; the second was to draw a sports day.

The class hated the first, but I was in heaven. Doing this mosaic of colours and shapes was the easiest thing in the world. I had never before experienced such a deep sense of satisfaction, and I remember thinking wistfully, 'I wish I could do this forever!'

As for the Sports Day, I solved its problems by employing a bird's eye view; making a flat green rectangle for the field and stick figures for the athletes. It so happened that at that particular time I was under a *kherem* or 'shunning' (it was a fad – sooner or later everyone had to undergo it). But when my drawing appeared on the school billboard all my friends, one by one, 'crossed the line' to have me do for them just such a picture. My talent had become a return ticket to society.

That year, in the final report card, I got a miraculous 'Excellent' in art, but my mother was not impressed. Art meant nothing, she said, my mark in Tanakh was very poor; I'd better begin to study or else.

Growing up, I watched as Hanania's art evolved into his own distinct style; stark forms, abstracted linear images of people and animals – mostly in black against a white background. His art was not easy (often kibbutz members puzzled over his holiday decorations for the dining-hall), but for me it stood for everything art should be; integral, resolute, enigmatic, and sublime. How then could I dare dream of becoming an artist? All the questions and all the answers were embodied in my brother's work. Hanania's was an impossible act to follow.

One reads of chance encounters people had had in their youth that revealed to them their true vocation, thereby changing the course of their life forever. Come to think of it, I too had such an encounter – only I didn't have the wits and the courage to follow it.

I was twenty when the Helena Rubinstein Museum in Tel-Aviv staged a major exhibition of European abstract art. It was the first of its kind in Israel, and caused heated debates for and against abstraction.

As for me, that first visit to the gallery was an epiphany. I was in a daze, and turning around and around taking it all in, I felt as if I had come home; as if these large paintings, with their bold forms, their intense colours, and their lack of subject matter, were mirrors reflecting my soul. I longed to be able to paint that way – if only I were an artist…

But I wasn't; and with zero faith in myself and in my run-of-the-mill talent, I blocked all the roads that could have led me in that direction. Ever since my childhood I was familiar with the works of all the great masters of the past; the crucifixions, the Madonnas, the saints, the portraits, the Venuses, the landscapes and the still lives. There was nothing one could add to this canon. Therefore there was no point in going to school to study art, since today's artist had to be endowed with a gift that was more than skill. Had I such a gift I would already have done original work that would have emerged from an inner place, like music or poetry. To reproduce the visible was anecdotal and redundant. Besides, nature is too vast and changeable; I could never presume to capture its true likeness; and even though Turner and the Impressionists had done it, I would have nothing new to say. Thus, not wishing to apply myself to the latter and unable to do the former, and with the advent of the guitar, I eventually stopped doing art altogether.

And then, without asking for it, in my third year of doing latihan, I received the gift. One Saturday morning, busy around the flat, I got a peculiar feeling that I should stop everything I was doing, and do art instead; the feeling was accompanied by a strong inner vibration, similar to a latihan, though I was not in latihan. So I hauled out from the bottom of the closet the old cardboard box with my art supplies, sat down at the kitchen-table, paper and crayons in front of me, and waited. My last painting, which I had done years ago, was a 'pretty' Renoir kind of landscape. I didn't expect anything better now. I felt a tingling in my fingertips and my hand reached out to pick a crayon (a cayenne blue) and began to draw across the paper with deliberate strokes. Shapes materialized; other colours followed (not necessarily of my choice); finer details added – and, voila`, the drawing was finished. Throughout the experience I remained detached and uninvolved, like a spectator. The final result, a Kandinsky like abstraction, had good balance and energy; above all it *felt* real – unlike my usual efforts, which always seemed contrived.

I have never lost that initial sense of wonder, but soon I learned that the gift was not a toy. I wanted to believe that this art I was producing was the language of my soul, but was it? Also much as I gained familiarity with it, I didn't know what I was doing and what it all meant. I liked the end results, but couldn't help doubting the validity of this 'automatism'. Was it me who did it, or was I only a channel for something else? How could I claim this art as mine?

Periodically in the ensuing five years I would be 'visited' by these impulses. They came with the changing seasons, like migrating birds in autumn, like the pelting rains in winter, or the wild flowers in early spring; and left as abruptly! It was fantastic when it happened; but as one cannot tame a flock of birds, or harvest wild flowers, so I couldn't harness this gift. Thus I had no cause to become too eager, proud, or possessive. Frankly the gift was, as yet, too big for me. As Bapak had explained, I was given a Cadillac but didn't know how to drive, and had no garage to house it in.

Therein also lay my frustration. Any artistic endeavour requires skill, and any skill needs a teacher. But none of the teachers I approached could help me. When I showed my work to the painter Ruth Bamberger, she exclaimed, 'you are a natural, my teaching will only get in your way.'

While another artist, Joram Rozov, the dean of Bezalel School of Art, looked silently through my work, saying finally, 'you could benefit from some drawing classes...I am giving an introductory course this summer...'

I took classes with both. With Mrs. Bamberger I learned the basics of handling oil paint, and with Mr. Rozov I drew meticulous life drawings, working many hours, with many types of pencils, on the perfect shading of an elbow. It was undoubtedly not a waste of time but as far as my soul drawings were concerned it was for the birds and didn't make a jot of difference. In truth, all the art classes I took, then and later in Canada, have had little bearing on the other way of working. In the end I would have no teachers except my inner guidance and myself.

Consequently in those early years my faith in my new potential was fragile, and when my life became disrupted again, it was this gift that went into hibernation.

Like A Cow in The Meadow

'The guidance you receive in the latihan comes from your own nature. It is really in line with your ability and character.

'For example: you have the nature of a farmer and should have become a farmer, but you have instead become a secretary, or architect, or businessman. When you work you never have a feeling of satisfaction. You never have a feeling that you can give a hundred percent of everything to your work. And this affects your outer circumstances, your earning capacity, your ability to take care of your livelihood, etc.

'Even those of you who, in doing wrong work, work that is not in line with your own capacity and talent may earn well -- you may get a good job and earn plenty of money, yet, you never feel satisfied.

'You always feel like a bird in a cage. You never feel free.

'This is the importance of the spiritual training. Gradually, bit-by-bit, you can receive for yourself what is the right work, the way of working that suits your own inner nature. Gradually you can find the field of work that is really in line with yourself, with your inner nature. So that when you work you will feel a hundred percent satisfied. You will have a feeling of love for your work to the extent that, whatever you are working on, you feel as though you are working on your own property. You will always feel you are working for yourself. And this is one benefit of the latihan kedjiwaan. It is important that you be aware of it and really put your latihan into practice.'

Muhammad Subuh Sumohadiwidjojo, from a talk given in Los-Angeles 22.07.81

July 1981, Vancouver, Canada; Bapak is testing with the ladies questions revolving around work: how does a secretary work; a nurse; a teacher? I am thinking, 'Ugh, here we go again; typical female jobs!'

More testing: how does a ballerina work? Bapak chuckles and Sharif translates; 'This is a good exercise for the heavier ladies among you...' As I am standing in the front row I blush; I take it personally.

The questions take a somewhat new direction (has he read my mind?): how does an architect work; a doctor; and last, how does a painter work?

'This is for me!' I think, 'now I'll find out if I am on the right track.' But nothing happens. As I stand and wait, I become aware that I am looking intently at something in front of me – as if at a canvas on an easel; I am taking my time studying it, and then, with deliberate movements, I begin to put a dab of paint here and a dab there, stepping back to check the results…

'So this is how a real painter works,' I think, 'perhaps a Vermeer – but it isn't me. I work mostly with crayons and do quick, intuitive scribbles on paper. Clearly I am not an artist.' And I leave the testing discouraged and disappointed.

On that visit Bapak also urged the helpers to find their true talent:

'It is really important for you to know your own talent and to be able to answer members who have the same question…'

And immediately after that talk I cornered three helpers to test with me. It was urgent, I said, it couldn't wait. Thus when we finally got together, at the end of a day of fasting, before dinner and after a long and tedious helpers meeting, we just wanted to get on with it. The ladies didn't know me from Adam, yet there was little preliminary talk. I didn't tell them about myself, and they didn't ask. None of us had done this kind of testing before, yet we believed naively that if we placed our sincere trust in the Almighty, things would turn out all right. Only one question was asked, the big one: what was Silvana's true talent? Just like that – cold turkey. Not surprisingly the outcome was a total flop. The answers were all over the place; nothing was certain, nothing clarified, there was no follow up, and I went home royally confused and on the verge of a major crisis.

That was the time when the floodgates opened and talent testing became all the rage in Subud. And indeed there circulated some tantalizing stories about individuals who had received their true talent (TT) through testing, who had bravely turned their lives around to start out on a new and better path. I too persisted with my search, testing at every occasion, with any helper who came my way; invariably getting nowhere.

These are some of the gems I collected on my quest: My TT is to be a farmer and grow cabbages. (Imagine the crisis that got me into!) My TT is to worship God (yeah, sure). My TT is working with colourful fabrics; a seamstress maybe? (Getting warmer – I was a weaver at the time.) One helper announced unequivocally: 'No, art is not your talent, you are being pretentious,' then, relenting a little, 'but you are a real musician!' On that occasion I received that art was indeed my talent, but as no one received anything remotely close I lost heart again. Another time one helper assured me warmly: 'your TT is to be a mother!' And others said: 'we received a strong feeling about *something* but we don't understand what it means...' Only the late Isabel Prentice, God bless her, received clearly, 'it is about colours and it is very strong...' But I was too tense and received nothing.

At the 1983 Subud World Congress at Anugraha Conference Centre in Windsor, England, the international and national helpers offered to test the TT with whoever wished to do so, and there was a long line up of hopefuls who had signed up. As I was a newly appointed national helper, I joined one afternoon to learn how it was done. But after five gruelling hours I came to the conclusion that though the efforts were commendable, the results were negligible and ineffective. That the matter was too deep and too involved and couldn't be hastened; that it was in God's time and by His will; and that what we were doing was akin to a diviner searching for precious metals with a divining rod. And that was when I got off the merry-go-round and surrendered the whole shebang to Almighty God.

My grand epiphany happened two years later. It was a bright summer morning in June. I stood in the bathroom brushing my teeth and thinking; 'Didn't I read somewhere, in one of Bapak's talks, that working at one's true talent feels like a cow grazing in the meadow? Right, like a cow! This must be one of Bapak's jokes! I do not have affinity to, and don't understand cows. Bapak, you lost me there! Okay, don't fight Bapak but give him a chance. Now what will happen if I let myself feel this cow in the meadow? Why not test it?'

So there and then I tested how it felt to be a cow grazing in the meadow and, behold, it was a fantastic receiving. To be like a cow in the meadow is to be in a most natural and contented state; bless the cow! It is an existence in the here and now where there are no doubts, no questions and no striving; it is a state of perfect harmony.

Now that I had the perfect paradigm I went on to test how my particular talents stood in comparison. Testing about the music revealed what I had always known; music is indeed very good, but it centres in my head and my heart; the ease and naturalness of the grazing cow is missing. The weaving, which had given me so much satisfaction in the last eight years, wasn't bad either; yet there was something affected and superficial about it; it lacked integrity. But when it came to painting, there were no reservation and no qualifications; the receiving went far beyond the peaceful cow and was an indescribable, all-embracing homecoming.

And so, overcome by emotions, tears running down my face, I stood in the sun-drenched bathroom as if on a stage flooded with light and at my side stood my long neglected life as an artist. At last, at the age of 47, I was ready to embrace it, bring it to the forefront, and accept the responsibilities and challenges that it entailed.

***

I woke up early today. My husband had just left for work (the alarm clock pointed to 5:14), but instead of going back to sleep I became wide-awake: where do I go from here in my story? What else is there to tell? Like always I feel obliged to defend my claim to the title Artist as if I am required to provide some proof of an early precociousness. 'But it is really such a meagre crop,' I think 'a short CV on one page should do…'

'Don't be a cynic!' chided Inner Voice.

At that moment a strange thing happened; out of the darkness, from the far corner of the bedroom, came flying a whirlwind of images, like pieces of a huge puzzle, moving with great velocity, like a movie on fast-forward, assaulting me like a swarm of bees, circling and attacking my head. I recognized them at once as pictures from my life. This was my whole life's story! Goodness, this fragment belongs too and that one…how blind can one be!

The experience ended abruptly, and I was back in the dark bedroom. Of course any remnant of sleep was gone and I got up. The house was dark and cold. I turned on all the lights, raised the thermostat, and made myself a coffee. The memory of the images was fading fast, the way dreams do. But then the top of the puzzle re-appeared, that pale mauve horizon of my childhood, the gently undulating range of the Sumerian hills, the rosy morning sky, the ripening rye fields receding into the distance. I didn't understand the meaning of the image and had no desire to speculate. I would let the story unfold any which way it wanted.

Blue Rectangle

1. Gabbeh

I wouldn't have told this story if it weren't for the rug. A small blue Gabbeh rug I had recently purchased in IKEA. It was love at first sight in the store, but at home it lost its appeal. Feeling guilty – it had been a typical case of impulse buying – I wanted to return it.

'No, keep it,' said Inner Voice.

'But it isn't that spectacular, and it wasn't that cheap,' argued Head.

'Keep it, it has a meaning.' insisted Inner Voice.

Perplexed I studied it from every angle, dragging it from one spot to another (the thing is heavy), detecting none.

Only on the following morning, in the shower, a memory hit me, like a stone hitting the water – with a big splash. Goodness! This is *my* blue rectangle – the emblem I had devised for myself to represent the idea of beauty, creativity, and the eternal Grace, which had been inspired, in turn, by the sight of the *Ein-Avdat* pool I had visited 45 years ago, on that remarkable trip to the Negev.

I hurry down to the living room to have another look. And indeed upon closer inspection I see that what I had taken to be a uniform blue is in fact a striated surface that changes gradually from light to dark, from shallow to deep water, representing a pool framed by a yellow ochre desert. A herd of multi-coloured goats encircles it, and four animals have waded tentatively into its four corners. But there, in the middle, barely noticeable, swims one lone white kid. Instinctively I worry, is it in danger? What a foolish bold animal!

'What a find,' I think, 'here I have got myself a Gabbeh rug with a story!' Granted, it is a simple, everyday story about a reckless kid – it may have been the weaver's favourite – testing its independence in a pool on the desert plateau of Iran. But the imagery fits mine too. The pool is the said Ein-Avdat pool; I am the lone kid in the middle that in the future would, metaphorically, venture into the 'deep'; the four goats are the reluctant companions with whom I visited the place, and the herd represents itself – The Herd – which I have strained to get away from for most of my life.

I am amazed at the way this book is unfolding; how time and again I am given signs that in this undertaking I am not alone and that this enterprise is not by my design only.

2. Yom Kippur

All told, 1963 was not a good year. I was back in Beit-Yitzhak living with my mother. I had survived the break-up of an obsessive and hopeless love affair; I had muddled my way through the first year of teaching, but the future looked bleak and I doubted I'd survive a second year.

It was late September, and the Jewish High Holidays of Rosh Hashanah, Yom Kippur and Succoth, which fall at the beginning of the school year, were a perfect respite.

On Yom Kippur eve I went to Tel-Aviv to visit my friend Ze'ev. We were to be four: Ze'ev, his girlfriend Ya'el, his best friend and boss, John, and I. The general idea was to liven-up the day and be in good company. None of us intended to fast.

My friendship with Ze'ev started in 1959 when he came to Beit-Yitzhak looking for work. I had been working that summer in the Post Office and when he entered for the first time I thought. 'Hullo! A new face – and handsome too! Girls must fall for you; but I won't... you are not my type.' He had the Tom Cruise kind of looks, a strong pleasant face, athletic, and moving with a certain grace, like a dancer

In the afternoon my mother informed me she had a new tenant and that she and I would have to share one bedroom again. And when I answered the door that evening there he stood, that handsome young man from the Post Office. His first words, to the side, were not promising; 'I hope it isn't always so messy here.' I blushed; my mother was notoriously untidy. But contrary to first impression, Ze'ev turned out to be a model lodger. He had excellent rapport with my mother, he loved dogs and helped with the chores; in short, he became like one of the family.

A year later, after the break-up with my boyfriend, Ze'ev became my confidant, my best friend and, eventually, my lover. By then he had left the dairy farms for computer programming, and there was even talk of marriage. But though he was a true friend, I didn't love him enough to marry him. He was too much of an open book, too much like putty in my hands, and instinctively I knew that this was not conducive to lasting respect. Above all, I was not ready. I had barely opened my eyes to the world and there was this something I had to find. I needed freedom to keep searching. Ze'ev said he would wait; and though he had had a string of girlfriends, of whom Ya'el was the latest, he implied that if only I'd give the sign he would drop everything for me.

Now I was meeting John for the first time. I have heard much about him; that he was a computer whiz and a brilliant chess player; that he was somewhat younger than Ze'ev; in fact that he was the youngest boss in that company; also that he had been exempted from the army because of a disability.

When John opened the door for me I immediately tensed up; he looked so much like my brothers. His slender body and slight shuffle reminded me of Hanania, his calm, intelligent face and blue eyes of Stephan and his reticence and dry sense of humour of both. Above all he was a mystery and I couldn't resist the attraction, despite knowing full well that it wouldn't do. He was Ze'ev's best friend, and Ze'ev, though practically engaged to Ya'el, still guarded me jealously as if I were his property.

Ya'el couldn't join us after all, and since Yom Kippur brings the city to a virtual stand-still, the three of us remained housebound whiling away the hours playing games, listening to music, eating the excellent food Ze'ev's sister had left for us and, on the spur of the moment, planning a trip to the Negev for the coming weekend of Succoth. The four of us (Ya'el didn't like roughing-it-out, but Ze'ev would talk her

into it) in John's old Ford   yes, it can make it   all the way south to the
beaches of Eilat.

3. The Betrayal

Forty years ago I tried to write down this story, but it eluded me as I
kept getting lost in its details and emotional quagmire. Even now I fail
to understand its importance; why has it remained so vivid in my
memory? And why do I feel that it is a riddle I am required to solve?

First, however, I have to come to grips with the betrayal. It is
remarkable that all the years of doing latihan have done nothing to
remove its sting; I am still smarting as if it had happened yesterday.

But after lunch, on the verge of dozing off in the big armchair, I
receive an answer when a forgotten memory flashes before my eyes. I
am ten years old. It is evening. I am jogging along the main village road.
As I pass the Rosenberg farm, their large yellow dog, which had been let
off its chain, comes charging at me, barking menacingly. Though I am a
dog person, I am wary. This one has a nasty reputation. I slow down,
face it, and order it to go home... It retreats and I resume my walk with
deliberate calm. But it returns with reinforcement – a few smaller,
harmless dogs, all barking from a safe distance. As the yapping reaches a
frenzied crescendo, Yellow, emboldened, suddenly strikes, sinking his
teeth into my leg. All I remember after that is the sight of the little
dogs, guilt ridden, scurrying away in all directions.

So here is clue number one! The betrayal was on a par with the
behaviour of dogs – in other words, it was on the animal level! I laugh
out loud and the bitterness vanishes miraculously. The picture begins to
come into focus.

On the morning of the appointed day, on the way to Tel-Aviv, I begin
to feel uneasy. Maybe the whole thing is a big mistake. One would need
a magician to make it work. This infatuation with John is madness; I
should heed my inner warnings. Besides, John is holding his cards close
to his chest and I could easily get hurt. And how will I accommodate
Ze'ev who doesn't deserve to get hurt either? And what about Ya'el

whom I scarcely know? I met her only once and though I liked her, we had little in common; she was younger and seemed in awe of me, even though she herself had the advantage of being a tall, slim, reddish-blond, green-eyed beauty. And then there was the pact Ze'ev and I had made to tone down our sibling-like bantering so that Ya'el wouldn't feel left out. Thinking about it, I experience the sinking sensation I get when I do something wrong. I don't know why, yet the more I think about the whole venture the less I like the looks of it. But now it's too late, and shrugging off these doubts, I let the thought of seeing the Negev overrule any misgivings.

Apparently I wasn't the only one who had second thoughts. Ze'ev, who met me at the door, looked oddly sheepish; there had been a last minute change of plans, he said, a fifth person was to join us, a classmate of John's, by the name of Ruth. I smelt a rat; I should have been consulted, let alone informed; but I suspended my anger. In the car, on the way to pick her up I sensed a general embarrassment but then, when I saw her, my heart sank and I knew I had been betrayed - 'The Philistines are upon you!'

For an instant I wanted to stop the car and go home; but I didn't. Deep down I felt that this was something I had to go through, by hook or by crook, even though the prospect of sharing four days with this young woman, now scrambling cheerfully into the back of the car, was enough to make me cry. The antagonism was mutual and instantaneous – I had met my nemesis.

She was the kind of person I'd try to avoid at all cost; the narrow-minded, vulgar busybody. She had nothing to redeem her, no kindness, intelligence or wit, only cunning and mistrust. There wasn't much to her looks either: small eyes, puffy face, kinky hair, and a matronly figure. Was there any reason for John to invite her other than to act as a watchdog? And was this the best he could come up with? How I had misjudged him! It was that unfortunate family resemblance that had tricked me; John the deep was merely an immature and insecure boy!

We were less than half an hour on the road, when Ruth jabbed at my shoulder, announcing, 'by the way, I want you to know that we are not *dreaming* of hiking with you in the desert. You must be out of your mind – in that heat? If you want to hike, do it alone! *We* won't hold you back... ha, ha'.

She was referring to the plans we had made on Yom Kippur when I talked the guys into taking a short hike in the vicinity of Eilat. Her unprovoked rudeness caught me off guard, but I was more astonished that no one challenged it – in fact that no one said a word. That's when it dawned on me that this was a conspiracy. Granted, Ruth was the wild card and her arrival was bound to change the dynamics of the group, placing me in the doubtful position of a fifth wheel. But any hope I had for equilibrium was shattered when, from the moment she set foot in the car, she took upon herself to guard the others against my machinations. After all it was I who was the odd one out.

Thus without warning and for no apparent reason, I became a pariah, and even Ze'ev turned his back on me. He avoided eye contact and ostentatiously lavished his attention on poor Ya'el, making a farce of our agreement. I sat in the front seat beside a frigid John who, ignoring me rudely, directed his undivided attention on the rear mirror, on Ruth and her wiles. And she, like a terrier, kept worrying that tired bone, that desert hike, which for the rest of the day formed the central theme that fed the flames of her hilarity.

Behind me there was whispering and snickering; but when I attempted to say something neutral my words were met with awkward silence or sneers. The situation was surreal, and laughing darkly, I imagined myself the femme fatale in a French film noir, Jeanne Moreau in 'Jules et Jim'.

We travelled for hours, the landscape changing rapidly from the lush green of orange groves to the sun-baked expanses of the Negev. In the back Ruth held Ya'el captive under her spell, overruling Ze'ev's growing uneasiness; and in the front John, sunglasses hiding his eyes, remained inscrutable. I squeezed as far as I could against the door, leaning my face out the window into the hot wind, my hair whipping across my burning eyes, contemplating the fundamental loneliness of human existence.

4. The Blue Rectangle

We stopped for the night in the historic Nabatean town of Avdat. A spectacular sunset lit the sky as we followed the guide among the ruins; but in the gathering purple it was evident that the situation had not changed: Ze'ev continued to shun me, pompously soliciting Ya'el who wasn't fooled and seemed unhappy and insecure. To her credit she did try to exchange a few civil words with me, but she was shy and hesitant. Ruth, having lost interest in her nipping game, forgot about me altogether and bustling jovially, chaperoned a placid and contented John, the two couples keeping each other company. And I, strolling fifty paces behind, kept fortifying my own bubble of solitude.

Early next day we left the paved road and drove out into the desert in search of the famed Ein-Avdat pool. Driving for what seemed an eternity through the monotonous, arid expanses of the Avdat plateau, clouds of white dust threatening to choke the engine, the unforgiving earth extending as far as the eye could see – the idea of finding water, let alone a pool, seemed inconceivable.

Yet, unexpectedly there we were; standing on a ridge looking down a deep canyon and onto the incredible sight of a large, elongated pool hewn into the sheer desert rock. To see this unlikely expanse of shimmering, deep blue was to witness a miracle; but entering it was like entering a shrine.

The others remained sitting on the rocks; only Ze'ev swam out once to meet me in the middle, wordlessly asking for forgiveness. But nothing mattered anymore, the unfortunate trip, the unaccountable betrayal. The cool water washed away, as if with an invisible hand, the pettiness, the anger, the humiliation, and in their stead I was left empty and peaceful. And suspended in this timeless reality there arose in me an awareness of an all-encompassing presence that was like a silent pledge: I'll find in time that which I have to find, the source within me is alive.

5. Eilat

The beaches of Eilat teemed with vacationers and tourists. Released from the car's confinement and weary of two days of enmity, we simply did what everybody else was doing: swimming and hanging out on the beach. Somewhere between Ein-Avdat and Eilat I ceased to be an outcast and that evening, as we sat in the hostel cafeteria, tired and sunburned, yesterday's issues were forgotten and the affected coupling lost its raison d'être. The drama was over and nobody expected a sequel.

Then the door opened and a tall, gangly, young man entered, his backpack hanging casually off one shoulder, a tourist no doubt, easily recognizable by his air of vagueness.

'Norbert!' I waved to him, 'what are *you* doing here?'

His face lit up as he strolled over to our table, and instantly the mellowing atmosphere became charged with crackling high voltage! An intruder and a foreigner! But Norbert, easygoing and relaxed, ignored it and guilelessly attempted to engage the others in a friendly conversation with his minimal Hebrew and their virtually non-existent English.

Norbert had visited me in Beit-Yitzhak in early July, having got my address from our mutual friend, Michal. He was studying art in London and had come to Israel to work on a Kibbutz and learn some Hebrew. He said he wanted to know enough to be able to read the first chapter of the Hebrew Bible in the original. The Hebrew words sounded so beautiful in their brevity: 'B'resheet Bara Elohim...'

Norbert had a boyish round face with a fine beak nose, full lips, and round eyes. There was a permanent droll expression on his face like that of an astonished ten-year-old who is trying to figure out a joke. The rapport between us was immediate, as if he was my long-lost twin. We talked for hours, and when he left the next day I felt regret – we would probably never meet again. And here he was – cool and detached, with his little smile, like a strange bird that has flown in from the wild to roost among the pigeons.

Naturally I invited him to our bonfire and for tomorrow's trip to the Coral Beach, disregarding my companions' silent objections. Ze'ev's face darkened, he couldn't conceal his jealousy, while Ya'el observing him, understood and looked even more dejected. Ruth, who seemed to have lost all her zest – she had played her part and wasn't needed anymore, was clueless; she became invisible, like a forgotten piece of luggage in an airport terminal. John tried with his halting English to conduct a polite conversation, but they had nothing in common, so there was little to talk about.

And I, I had not the slightest doubt that Norbert's arrival on the scene was not a serendipitous coincidence but a deliberate move on the part of the Grand Scriptwriter. The sense of deliverance was absolute! Of course I had every reason to be elated. I would have Norbert's company for two more days and, having a partner, would regain my status as a person of consequence; besides, being an artist, Norbert was reinforcement in this covert mini-war of Philistines against culture. But beyond it all, there lingered an exquisite bright feeling, as if my insides were full with popping, evanescent bubbles of laughter, a laughter that was out of this world.

Next day we went on a hike after all, along a mountain trail in the southwestern region of Eilat, and the view, as I had promised, was superb. I say we, but I only remember walking alongside Norbert; Ze'ev and John kept their distance and Ya'el and Ruth stayed on the beach. As I 'paraded' my Negev to Norbert, he with his fresh eyes opened mine to beauties I had taken for granted: 'I can't get over this sky!' he marvelled, 'it is practically mauve!' (As far as I was concerned the sky was blue and there was nothing more to be said about it.)

Norbert, I believed, was a true artist. The world had more meaning and was more beautiful in his company; and I was readily falling in love again. That evening I left the deflated foursome to their devices and joined Norbert in his tent on the beach. They returned north early next day, while Norbert and I took our time and left later by bus.

We got off at Machtesh-Ramon to enjoy the Negev for one last time. The grand panorama of the crater-like formations lay before us and on its edge, like sentinels, complementing its rugged rocks, stood an installation of monumental sculptures. We soaked in the scenery, discussed the artistic merits of each sculpture, and I was in heaven; this was what my life should be all about – beauty and art.

The afterglow of another Technicolor sunset lit the Machtesh rim with a final kiss, fading into THE END. But the melancholy evening wind, sweeping over the open vistas, carried on its wings a faint tinkling of ironic laughter…

6. Post script

This morning while thinking about the story and its implications – for even after having written it, I still didn't have a clue what it was all about – I caught myself humming an old, forgotten ballad, which used to be very popular in my time. Slowly, and with relish I retrieved its verses from oblivion; when suddenly something clicked. What do you know? Here lies the answer, right in this ballad! How very funny and strange.

The Ballad, by the Israeli poet Nathan Alterman, is a nonsensical lullaby that goes somewhat like this: night after night you sit by the window and wait. The night is stormy. The wind moans in the treetops. And riding on the road are three armed cavalrymen.

> '…A beast the first devoured.
> …By the sword the second died.
> …And the one who did remain,
> Sleep my child, forgot your name.'

Three men! I have never considered this story from that angle – always too eager to be the one who had been wronged. Three unsuitable men indeed!

'A beast the first devoured' – That is simple; Ze'ev's name means Wolf. I kept in touch with him a while longer. Ze'ev married Ya'el eventually, after I went to England to join Norbert. Tragically Ya'el got killed in a motorcycle accident a few years later. Ze'ev visited me one more time in Jerusalem to introduce his new wife. He said she reminded him of me; and quietly aside he added, 'but you were my only love.'

'By the sword the second died' – That must be John the 'unapproachable' (think John the Baptist as in the play *Salome* by Oscar

Wilde). I never again saw or heard anything of him or Ruth. But I know now that the treachery was all John's doing. How do I know? A sudden 'threshold of revelation', that's how. It was John who masterminded the whole plot. Ruth had indeed been invited as a watchdog; John had known her from school and knew what she was capable of, and thus he set her on me – like that vicious yellow dog; but not to protect himself; what an idea! This was where I had made my big mistake! No, my feminine charms had no effect on John. But when he met me on Yom Kippur and saw the power I wielded over Ze'ev, he wanted me out of the way. He probably convinced Ze'ev that what he was about to do would be for the best, that I needed to be taught a lesson for the pain I caused Ze'ev with my thoughtless flirtation; when in fact John wanted Ze'ev for himself (Ya'el was never a threat). For John, the young promising boss, the master chess player and genius computer programmer, was in love with Ze'ev.

'And the one who did remain' – As told elsewhere, the relationship with Norbert didn't last. In reality he was too young and his equanimity, which had so attracted me to begin with, became later a liability. Once I left him I saw how I had confused my search for identity with love. He wasn't my 'other half', but a mirror in which I wanted to see myself; he was the artist I wanted to be. In fact while living with him I felt even more impoverished, like a starving pauper watching others stuffing their faces.

We stayed on friendly terms for a while longer, and then lost touch.

A week after I had destroyed Norbert's letters and artwork in that grand purge of 1973, I received a letter from him, from Sweden. He wrote that cleaning out drawers he came across my photograph, which brought back memories. We had had some good times together and he wondered how I was doing. He himself was divorced and had a child, etcetera... But I didn't appreciate being remembered only while clearing out rubbish, and wrote him a caustic reply. Upon which two months later I received his last communication: I had hurt his feelings badly but it didn't matter anymore for he had found peace and oblivion from the world and from people like me in a Buddhist temple in Japan.

The ballad ends thus:

> 'Night after night the wind is storming,
> Night after night the treetops are moaning,
> Night after night only you are awake,
> Sleep my child sleep, the road's desolate.'

PART FOUR
A NEW BEGINNING

Shlichey Mitzvah Lo Nizokim

In the dream I am navigating a canoe on a fast river. Erica, a Subud sister from Tel-Aviv, is sitting behind me paddling. We are caught in a powerful current and are being swept towards a high wall of rocks. A crash is inevitable and I know we are going to die. At that moment I remember to direct my awareness inwardly to invoke the name of God. At once a powerful latihan takes over. It fills me with strength; I am fearless and in control. I succeed in turning the canoe 180 degrees away from the wall and we find ourselves rocking gently in calm water.

The accident happened a week later. We were on our way to Tel-Aviv to attend a Subud Israel AGM – five ladies in Vardina Sold's car. I sat in the front beside Vardina. Just as we left the outskirts of Jerusalem, a rear tire exploded with a loud bang, sending the car lurching all over the highway. Vardina, an experienced driver, held on to the steering wheel for dear life, struggling to regain control over the runaway car, which didn't respond but kept flying down the mountain gathering momentum. Ahead lay a sharp turn in the road and behind loomed a wall of rocks. There was no possible way the car could negotiate this turn in that speed. We were bound to crash into the wall.

Strangely calm, I asked silently, 'So is this *it?*' Receiving a decisive 'No'! As a powerful latihan grabbed my inside, holding me tight like a vise. Vardina turned and turned the steering wheel with all her might – like a captain working to steady a ship in a violent gale, while I, beside her, sat stock-still, praying silently, 'Allah, Allah...' aware that I am a channel, and that this intense latihan was not mine but hers. At the bottom of the road, missing the wall by a hair's breadth, Vardina stabilized the car, and it came to rest in the middle of the highway facing the oncoming traffic.

Being early Saturday morning the highway was deserted. We were safe, but for a few bumps and bruises.

Just then a lone tractor-trailer came puffing up the mountain. Seeing us stranded the driver stopped and offered his help. He changed the tire and checked the engine, all the while shaking his head in disbelief: what a miracle! Did we know how lucky we were to be alive?

I remembered the dream on the following morning. The image of the wall we missed brought it back. It was the same wall. Erica easily doubled for Vardina (both have large families and a similar astrological sign), and the latihan, which was the centre of the dream, was identical in strength, clarity, and purpose to the one I experienced in the accident.

We never discussed the event, and I told no one about the dream – the experience was too overwhelming. Yet I never doubted that its purpose was to guide and not to forewarn; that it was a training, or, if you like, a dress rehearsal!

It is tempting, here, to raise philosophical questions concerning Providence, Fate, Free Will, and the power of the latihan; but I am not in a position to elaborate on such matters. I leave that to the learned reader who is so inclined. I only described the experience to the best of my ability.

Working on the story, it occurred to me that after 30 years it was time that I told Vardina about the dream; after all it was her story too. Emailing obliged us to correspond in English, which made the communication somewhat awkward.

Vardina wrote back graciously that she remembered the accident well, and added, '...we were really very, very lucky! We also got all the help we needed after the accident. I thought we were protected because we were on our way to a Subud meeting and to latihan: *"Shlichey mitzvah lo nizokim"*, [meaning, those who are on an errand of Good Deeds will not be harmed.] I didn't know you had a dream ... maybe your dream predicted the path that led you far away from here…and I am sure that your latihan helped me in this very tense moment…

'Be well my sister,
Vardina.'

Beyond The Breakers

Jerusalem was the city of my choice ever since I had first visited it on a
school trip in grade seven and had vowed that one day I would make
it my home. I loved that city, its beauty, its climate and its light and
believed I could live there the rest of my life.

But after a few years in Subud there appeared signs to indicate that
something was not quite right, that this exquisite tapestry was frail and
fraying at the edges. There were times when I felt strangely heavy and
uneasy for no apparent reason; as if I had absorbed the heaviness of this
hallowed ground, so saturated with blood; as if I carried on my chest its
holy stones, imbibed with the possessive love that had been holding this
city captive for millennia.

And then one day, looking out from my balcony over the panoramic
view of the distant hills, I had a sudden premonition that this was not
the place where I would spend the remaining years of my life. That I
would have to move again and, what's more, that I would have to leave
Israel for good.

That was disconcerting. I loved the land. Also my life was settled
and comfortable; why leave? But as the feeling persisted, I tested with
the helpers and we received that indeed I would have to leave Israel
eventually; but 'not yet! Wait!' which was a relief – or rather a
reprieve...

Bloody history and heavy feeling aside, there was one obvious reason
for going into exile. I was single, in my mid-thirties, with no prospect of
finding a husband in the small community of Subud Israel. To marry
someone not in Subud was not an option. Life is complicated enough as
it is, I am complicated, and by all accounts marriage is complicated.
Without the latihan to bind us, the odds were strongly against such a
union. Which didn't leave me much choice: if ever I hoped to have a

family, I would have to pack my bags and seek this elusive husband in the big wide world – a needle in a haystack.

Every six months or so I repeated the testing, receiving, invariably, the same 'not yet'! But as patience is not my forte and as I had to do something, I did a kind of fast or *prihatin* (an Indonesian word that in the Subud context implies self-denial with an attitude of surrender to bring about a change in one's fortune): cutting back on sleep, avoiding sugar, abstaining from meat and having only one meal a day. The outcome was that I lost a lot of weight and never looked or felt better!

But I did not write to Bapak, knowing intuitively that his answer would only cause bigger problems in the long run. This road I had to follow at my own pace, in my way, and in God's time.

Then, one morning in early June of 1976, while sweeping the living room, I heard a voice, a distinct male voice saying, 'England!'

I stopped dead in my tracks; I had never heard such a 'real' voice before. It sounded as if somebody had spoken directly into my ear.

'Go to England!' repeated the voice with finality. My heart sank; I had been to England only the previous year and had no wish to go there again. Besides, I had already booked a tour to the Sinai, which meant last minute cancellation and awkward explanations. And what would I do in England, for heaven's sake? Yet the voice didn't leave room for negotiation; I had to obey.

A Subud musicians' conference in Kenfield Hall, advertised in the Subud U.K. newsletter, gave me a legitimate excuse for travelling, and I registered and purchased my flight ticket. But in July a telegram arrived – the conference had been cancelled. Now what? And just days before my departure I received an express letter from Loudwater, where I had hoped to stay for a while. The helpers there had taken the liberty to test on my behalf and received that I should stay in Loudwater only for a weekend, and that I should remain for the greater part of my vacation at Kenfield Hall.

I was incensed, I wasn't good enough for them, and perplexed: this venture was becoming more absurd by the minute. Nevertheless I did not cancel the trip. Something was afoot and I had to find out what it was.

With guitar, sketchbook and crayons, I arrived to a hot and parched England; I had never seen it so yellow. I stayed the prescribed weekend in Loudwater; I visited London and Bristol; but for the remaining fortnight I sojourned at Kenfield Hall, as I had been 'advised'.

Kenfield Hall, an estate situated some miles outside Canterbury, is a handsome country house (c. 1700) with lovely grounds and an impressive arboretum. However at the time of my visit it was under constructions and more like an empty shell – its splendour long gone. No one lived there but the caretaker and his young family. Occasionally it was being used for Subud U.K. functions, and one of its newly renovated wings served as latihan premises for the Canterbury group.

I was virtually the only guest. It was peculiar being in this large and empty place, alone, with no purpose and nothing to do. Naturally I strained against this 'edict'; why not visit Scotland instead? But at that point I didn't dare take the initiative without receiving His approval, and the test was clear: stay put!

People came for latihan on appointed nights; once I was invited to the gracious home of the writer Dominic Rieu. Lucia and her boys came down for a day, and occasionally a Subud member stopped over for the night. Nothing else interrupted my solitude. The room I slept in was large and sparsely furnished; I had to traverse a long corridor to reach the bathroom, and at night the creaking and rumbling of the old house made me fancy ghosts haunting the empty halls. During the days I took long walks in the estate grounds or the surrounding countryside; twice I got into town to visit the famed Canterbury cathedral. Daily I played my guitar and sketched. The fast of the Ramadan started [1] and the drought continued. I gave in to the rhythm of the place and stopped pushing; I had no further questions.

I have this image of walking in a field amongst Queen Anne's lace and chicory, tired and hot after a particularly ambitious trek. It must

---

[1] Bapak had recommended the fast for all Subud members. It was not only a requirement for Muslims, he said, but necessary for humanity. Fasting could bring us closer to our spiritual core and therefore closer to God.

have been noon, because I remember seeking the little shade that could be had along a hedge of brambles, when I had this startling thought.

'Before long you will leave Israel. You'll be living in a solitary place with no public transport (somewhat like this place here); therefore it is important that you start taking driving lessons!'

Since I had a mortal fear of driving and had vowed *never ever* to learn to drive, I had not a shred of doubt that this was a genuine, bona fide receiving.

And that is how I received the 'go ahead' signal. Quite an ingenious move, if you think about it, to send me all the way to England and onto the oddest retreat to receive it. For at home there were too many ties that held me back. One doesn't just up and go into exile without a good reason, and as long as I was under the spell of Israel and Jerusalem, there was no chance that I'd tear myself away.

But there was another important reason why I had to receive the signal alone, away from my friends and my Subud community, a reason which I understood much later. For the step I was about to undertake demanded my absolute and unalloyed conviction. No one should help another make that kind of decision (above all not the helpers), so that no one would be blamed or held responsible if things turned out badly or not as expected!

Accordingly, what impressed me most was how fearless and clear I felt about this new development! It was that which convinced me beyond doubt that I was ready!

The first of September was my last day in England. There was still time in the morning to go with Lucia to see a show of North American quilts London was raving about. At the time I didn't know much about quilts and was duly impressed. But there was more to this exhibition than Crazy Quilts. For while walking through the galleries I had the oddest feeling that there was something else I should be paying attention to, as though the quilts were telling me something – like when a friendly stranger gives you a knowing wink, and you think, 'am I missing something?' That day it began to rain, the drought was over, and that too had a special meaning, even the rain carried a personal message just for me…

Back from England, my first task and, as it turned out, the easiest, was to tackle those dreaded driving lessons. So much for mortal fear! Naturally I tested with the helpers to confirm the 'green light', but as to my destination I was advised to leave testing alone since it was (supposedly) a practical question that required practical handling. But I had not the foggiest idea how to proceed. There was no place in the whole world I wanted to go to, only the knowledge that I had to go, that I was ready, and that time was running out.

My first step was a round of letters to Subud members I knew in various countries, asking for their input. I didn't have much faith in this step and indeed it seemed to lead to nowhere seeing that all the replies were discouraging: 'we don't recommend…' 'You'll have daunting language problems…' 'Recession…' 'I feel that it is not the right place for you…' 'Do you really believe you could live here?

Only one reply failed to come – that from Canada. Already I had given up and was trying to re-assess my options, when the long-awaited letter arrived. Ramsey Oren, a Canadian citizen, who at one time had been a member of Subud Jerusalem, apologized: he had moved twice since, and my letter had gone astray. He then went on to paint in glowing colours my prospects in Canada, particularly Toronto. He believed that it was just the place for me; it was an important centre for the classical guitar, the home of a prominent guitar teacher, Eli Kassner, an ex-Israeli, whom I should contact immediately. He also suggested that I enrol in the University of Toronto to ease my entry process, and assured me that a Subud sister, Darlene, had offered me her hospitality when I arrived.

Suddenly everything fell into place. How strange that of all the countries in the world it was Canada, which had never excited my curiosity, which I had written off years ago, when I heard it described by an expatriate as being a dreary place, with no culture of its own and no history to speak of. I knew nothing about Canada; it was not a tourist destination, there was no readily available information; and all I could find in the book store were two patronizing, second-hand, tourist books written by Americans for Americans.

Also Canada had long acquired the dubious distinction of being a magnet for fortune hunters who were looked upon as deserters. And the pundits didn't tire of repeating the worn joke about how God commanded Moses to take his people to Canada, the (true) promised land of milk and honey, but Moses, being hard of hearing, dragged the Children of Israel through the desert for forty years in order to reach the land of Cna'an; and for what? Ever since we had had nothing but trouble...

And yet wasn't it also what I had been receiving in the latihan for months, 'Cana'a...Cana'a...' all the while wondering why on earth would I be repeating the word 'Cna'an'?

Again, testing about Canada was a mere formality since I had no doubts, but we tested nevertheless so the helpers could witness the rightness of my move. There was present at that session a visitor, Mariam Temple from Wollongong, Australia, who suggested I test also about Australia, 'we would love to have you...' It was tempting, that sunny continent with its friendly people, kangaroos, and deserts – but no! The strong feeling I had about Canada could not be trifled with; and after we all received that expansive feeling of growth and of giving thanks, there were no more questions.

There was a palpable sense of direction during those two years, the last in Jerusalem and the first in Toronto. It was a unique time of remarkable dreams, chance meetings, and inexplicable happenings. I had a keen awareness of it being a focal point where the destiny lines of my past, present and future, converged in one powerful instance. Never again will I experience anything remotely like that.

Thinking about that intensity and buoyancy, I was reminded of the summer of 1954 when, at sixteen, I succeeded to overcome a deep-water phobia I had had ever since I was a child. I trained myself to become a strong swimmer and on weekends, when everybody else hung out on the beach, I would venture alone beyond the breakers, diving under the waves, one after another, until I reached open sea. It was exhilarating to swim far out so that I would lose sight of the beach, but also lonely and dangerous. What if I got a cramp? And there were jellyfish and undertows; and returning was always a struggle.

But of course, as everyone involved in such activities knows, you become addicted to the adrenaline and to the euphoria of infallibility; you believe that nothing can go wrong. It may be illogical, but reasoning has little to do with it.

When I set out on this journey, my lawyer, family members, and associates expressed their concerns: it was foolhardy! I was selling my home, giving up a good job, leaving behind friends, family and security, to go to God-knows-where-and-what. But I had no doubts and no fears. I was anaesthetized by my conviction that I was doing the right thing and following God's Plan; that I was in His hands and He would protect me; that everything was going to be all right.

Against The Odds

There was a sense of urgency to my venture that didn't let me wait the two years required to obtain an immigrant visa; I therefore entered Canada as a tourist believing that as I had previously gotten by in England, so I would manage in Canada. Thus, ignorant of the customs of the country and full of naïve confidence, I shipped ahead my personal effects and had no contingency plans; the Almighty will take care of me. And indeed for a whole year I was being looked after; from the day I landed in Toronto on August 13, 1977 to the day Edgar and I returned from our honeymoon in September 1978. But after that I came down with a thump and had to learn to drive again, literally and metaphorically, being spared none of the collisions, spinouts, dead ends and engine failures – like most everybody else.

Ramsey, Darlene and her two children (a girl of eight and a boy of nine) waited for me at the airport. It was good to see Ramsey again, and Darlene and I hit it off from the start. Darlene, a single mother, was the proprietor of a dress shop on Dundas Street West. I had visualized her living in a mansion – wasn't Canada the land of plenty? But Darlene lived in a small three-bedroom apartment above the shop, and had, in her generosity, offered to share with me her own bedroom-cum-living-room space.

Ramsey arrived next morning, bright and early, to take me downtown and show me around. We took the subway and got off at Museum station. Later I learned that a stone throw away, hidden behind the Royal Ontario Museum and the Planetarium, was the Music Faculty – which had been Ramsey's secret destination all along. He, however, opted for the roundabout scenic walk, and I, blissfully unaware of his sly tactics, marvelled dutifully at the green expanses, the university's grand pseudo-Gothic architecture, the large trees, and the many squirrels! When, pointing to a modest, modern building Ramsey said, 'by the way, this is the Music Faculty; just give me a second,' and he was gone; he returned holding some forms in his hand and a Cheshire cat smile on his face. 'Guess what?' he said. 'Enrolment is still open! They had a major computer breakdown in the spring and are still accepting applications!'

I don't remember anything else about that day, since Ramsey had robbed me of my serenity and thrust me into a whirlwind of conflicting issues. I didn't want to go to university. This was the reason why I had ignored Ramsey's suggestion in his famous letter. I was afraid; I didn't believe I was the scholarly type. I was too old. There would be language issues, and financially it would be a heavy drain on my resources. But I couldn't tell Ramsey any of it. So we sat in a café on Bloor St. and I tried to subdue my panic and study the forms. I would be required to pass entry exams and do an audition; I would have to provide documents which I didn't have with me; my music skills were rusty as was my playing … I had just arrived…I needed time to adapt… Everything was too daunting! And I strained against the whole idea, and resented Ramsey for springing it on me.

'Think it over,' he said mildly, as he took his leave.

But that evening Darlene and her children took me 'out' to introduce me to 'the most typical Canadian treat', the many flavours of Baskin & Robbins ice cream. The following day I had to chase down my luggage, which had gone missing. Also I did the Ramadan fast which made thinking difficult, and furthermore, being a visitor, I had no space of my own in which to 'think it over' – so I didn't.

The day after, too busy in the shop, and with her children restless and bored, Darlene asked me to take them to the Canadian National Exhibition. 'Don't worry,' she assured me, 'they know what they want to do and they will show you where to go…' So off we went to the EX where, amidst the crowds, the rides, the food court and the noise (yes, I was fasting), one child got herself lost. Three hours of frantic search later – while her brother, unconcerned about his sister's fate, kept whining that she did it on purpose to spoil his day – all ended well. She had indeed wandered off on purpose, to taste her independence. She went to watch a movie down by the lake, after which she asked a nice-looking grownup to take her to the lost and found, and waited calmly for her mother to reclaim her.

With such a commotion I only said, like Scarlet O'Hara, 'I'll think about it tomorrow.'

Next morning I woke up at 4:00 am, with the last image of a dream filling my head: a huge close-up of my father's face looking at me impassively. I hardly ever dream about my father and didn't need to be a genius to figure out that this one was as urgent a message as I could possibly get: Just get on with it and stop dilly-dallying! And without further ado I started to act.

I applied to the Faculty of Music and sent express letters to Israel for the required documents; I found a place to live in, a small attic apartment on a quiet street, not too far from Darlene; I practiced for the audition and had my first lesson with Eli Kassner; and whatever else.

After the audition, which I passed, as I was leaving the room, the dean said, 'are you aware how extraordinarily lucky you are? If it weren't for the freak breakdown of our computer system in the spring you wouldn't have been able to apply at such a late date!' Did I detect in his voice a trace of resentment?

I was officially admitted to the University on September 19. Bapak arrived in Toronto on September 20. As always Bapak's visit was an all-consuming event; but those early days of classes in the university, and the intensity that surrounded Bapak's visit, became part of one grand feeling that everything was moving along as it should.

When three months later I went to have my tourist visa changed to a student visa, the officer informed me that this was the last time such a change was possible; that henceforth any application for student visa had to be made from the land of origin. He stamped the passport and handing it back he smiled and said, 'you know, you are a very lucky woman!'

It was shortly after New Year's that I met Edgar for the first time. The occasion was a social event in the Toronto Subud hall. I sat next to Darlene, catching up on the latest, when I noticed someone I hadn't seen before. I thought, 'a pleasant-looking man; must be in his early thirties; a good open face…' and then I gasped, 'goodness, he is the spitting image of my old friend Ze'ev! Taller and broader, yet so amazingly familiar!

I whispered to Darlene, 'who is that man talking with Rolphe, is he a new member?'

'No, this is Paul Waniuk; he is from the London group.'

'What does he do?'

'I believe he is an engineer; he lives on a farm and is building himself a big new house.'

'Is he married?'

'No.'

As it turned out, Paul, who would later change his name to Edgar, was the guest-of-honour. He had just returned from seeing Bapak in Honolulu (he was prevented from seeing him in Toronto because of the apple harvest) and was to give a slide presentation about the visit.

Afterwards I went over to talk to him. As he had been billeted in Hawaii with a family I knew – I had a perfect conversation starter. What was said is of no importance, for when I looked up into his eyes it happened. Now, people talk of falling in love, of chemistry, of being struck by a thunderbolt and such. This one was like a homecoming; not simple or mundane, but almost otherworldly (I would remind myself of this experience later, whenever I had to face the unavoidable challenges of married life).

The situation was quite foreign. Had I followed my impulses, I would have, beyond doubt, initiated the next move. But I held back. I was not going to be responsible if this didn't work out. Paul was gone, and the inner command was to do nothing. Sometimes, on certain latihan nights, I would receive an intense and unfamiliar latihan – and those were the times when, unbeknown to me, he was in the hall doing latihan upstairs. We would meet on the way out and exchange shy greetings. He came to Toronto very seldom.

March was drawing to an end. I was busy with final exams and forgot about Paul. It was time to take stock of my situation. I had a little talk with the Almighty: 'Well, *Elohim*, as far as I am concerned I have done all I am able to do here; but now my money is running out and my student visa will soon expire. I will have to return to Israel. In any case, thank you for all the support, it was a good experience. But if you have anything else intended for me, it is now entirely in your hands...'

On April 1st I came up with plan B: I wanted to continue to study, but not music and not in Canada. I would return to Israel, rebuild my life, and then apply to the university there. Having made up my mind I immediately wrote a letter to a friend in Jerusalem asking for her input; I predicted that I'd be back in July if not sooner.

With the same resolve I went out to mail the letter. There was still ice and snow on the sidewalk, though officially it was spring. Coming back, as I went up the stairs, I heard the phone ring and caught it just in time.

'This is Paul Waniuk,' his voice was hesitant, formal. 'We met in the Subud Hall a few months ago...'

On our first date we went to an elegant restaurant with old-fashioned décor of gold and burgundy, starched waiters, thick carpets and a hushed atmosphere. Paul was not the conversational type but we told each other a little about ourselves and I found out that he too was a vegetarian, that we shared certain (important) likes and dislikes, and that his Chinese Astrology sign (very important) was the Fire Dog, the only sign compatible with my difficult Earth Tiger. I asked him how he had found out about Subud. His was a direct road. He had bought at a Loblaw's supermarket a book, *The New Religions* by Jacob Needleman in which there is a chapter dedicated to Subud. He was intrigued, looked for a contact number in the Toronto telephone directory, and in due time was opened.

But it was only on our second date, when he kissed me, that I *recognized* him. He was the man in a dream I had in Jerusalem the year before I left for Canada – the man I knew would be my husband!

I am going up the stone passage that connects the street I live on with the one above. I am on my way to the grocery store. It is midday and hot but the passage is pleasantly shaded by pine trees, and as I climb the stairs I watch the sun flecks dance and shimmer at my feet.

116

Next I am standing in the middle of an empty street facing the grocery store. The black asphalt is hot, the light is blinding, and the sun is beating on my head. Beside me stands my favourite dog, Bina, a silvery medium Schnauzer, and to my horror I see entangled in her beard a large, black scorpion. What to do? Just then a tall, broad-shouldered young man emerges from the store and approaches us. He has an open, pleasant face and kind eyes. He flicks the scorpion away with his large hand, just so, and then he takes me in his arms saying, 'welcome home'.

We were married at City Hall. Darlene and Rolphe were our witnesses and we had our reception at the Art Gallery of Ontario. I wore a simple white cotton dress with Palestinian embroidery, a gift from a Subud sister from Jerusalem. I doubted I would ever wear it (white is not my colour), but took it along anyway, on a hunch... Also, to honour my mother, I wore her amber necklace, which had been given to her by my father on their wedding day.

A nice ending, that... but a cold female voice of an immigration officer interjects:

'Not so fast lady! Do you mean to tell me that you had just met this guy in the spring and two months later you are engaged to him? And you want me to believe you? This is a convenience marriage so you can stay in Canada. I know your type; you'll divorce him within a year. I am sorry but I cannot extend your visa. You'll have to return to Israel.'

'How long before I can come back?'

'You will have to apply for an immigrant visa and your so-called fiancé will have to sponsor you; it will take at least two years.'

'But I can't wait that long, I am 40 and this is my last chance to have children!'

'Sorry, I can't help you.'

After some fretting I extended my student visa by re-applying to the university, and later, after we were married, a more sympathetic officer in a smaller town, granted me the hoped-for immigrant status – albeit not before subjecting me to the grilling of a panel of three interrogators who had come from Toronto specifically for that purpose.

On The Farm

This was another dream I had the year before my exodus.

I am in a large room with brown panelling and a polished wooden floor. The room is bare but for two bundles of sacking in the far corner. Suddenly the bundles begin to unravel, disclosing two ancient, shrivelled, people. The scene is terrifying. I turn away and see a sinuous old man standing in the doorway, brandishing his fist and shouting angrily. I know it is not directed at me yet I am petrified and dare not look back at the other bundle.

The dream remained a one-of-a-kind nightmare and meant nothing, unlike the way dreams usually do, enigmatic as they might be; until, that is, I met these people in the flesh. For just as one dream had shown me my future husband, this one 'unfurled' to me my future parents-in-law. Maybe the purpose of the dream was to confirm, though it didn't make things any easier. For in the end nothing could have prepared me for the shock of meeting them. They were so alien, so rugged and old – as if they had just stepped out of an old sepia photograph of peasantry in Czarist Russia. Only then did it dawn on me that Edgar was not free the way I was, and that if I hoped to build a future with him, I would have to share it with his parents too – literally. We would have to live together under one roof, since Edgar's home was theirs and since they were utterly dependent on him. The thought that these people would become part of my life (become my *parents*), the idea that I'd enter by my own volition their twilight zone, their dried-up life – demanded my last ounce of courage and more. I had made it so far.

It was my first visit to the farm. We entered the house, unceremoniously, from the veranda, through the sliding glass door that led directly into the dining room and the kitchen. Edgar, as the master of the house, tramped in unconcerned – hallooing cheerfully, but I wished for a somewhat more formal entry. His mother Anna stood by the kitchen sink. She was very old and very small, with an alarmingly bent back. As we were introduced she strained to straighten it and nodded a grudging welcome while eyeing me suspiciously. She had the look of a typical Russian babushka; high cheekbones, resolute chin, her thin, white hair gathered into a small knot at the back of her head. She was toothless and very pale and had, like Edgar, that curious ridge between the forehead and the nose; and though she was hostile, there was a spark in her eyes, which made me want to like her in spite of the mistrust.

Meanwhile, Edgar's father, Teodor, who sat facing an old black-and-white television, ignored us altogether. He didn't get up to greet me but threw us a dark look and, gesticulating with his hands, pointing to the screen, violently cursed, in Polish, the government, Prime Minister Trudeau, and the Jews (one needn't know Polish to understand that). Teodor was thin and wiry, his hair cropped closely to his skull, his unshaven, weather-beaten face, deeply troubled. Teodor didn't speak one word of English. Anna could communicate a little, but did not seem to understand when spoken to; and as the parents were hostile and as no civilities were offered, and as it was pointless to even try, I followed Edgar's example and ignored them, disconcerting as it was.

Ignoring people is a nasty art. But this was precisely what I had to learn in order to protect myself. Therefore when we planned our wedding it never occurred to me to invite the parents. Darlene, however, was appalled; being a proper Jewish daughter she could not imagine a wedding without the parents. 'You must invite them!' Consequently, guilt ridden and against my deepest instinct, I convinced Edgar to bring the old people along. But they didn't ask for it, and sitting among our friends they seemed lost and bewildered. Though in the wedding photograph it is only Teodor who looks lost; Anna is sitting ramrod straight, her chin stuck out defiantly, her expression resolute.

Edgar had built the new house with the optimism of a bachelor, hoping to have one day his own family and his parents all living together under one roof – one big, happy family. The house replaced the original small farmhouse, which had been carted away leaving behind its gaping foundation. The new house wasn't quite finished yet – the upper floor was only roughed in – but it promised to become a grand home with fieldstones and cedar shingles on the outside and generous spaces inside. And yet the house felt wrong, and everything in it appeared shabby and neglected. The walls were bare and most of the furniture was discarded hand-me-down. The living room (with hardwood floor, a large fireplace and French windows) was never used. The parents, if they were not working outside or watching television in the bare dining room, would huddle around the Formica table in the stark, over sized kitchen. Plainly the house was too big for them, too modern, too foreign, and they lived in it like squatters in a palace.

It was on one of my visits to the farm that Edgar proposed. According to the movies this should have been a romantic event with candlelight dinner and an engagement ring. And indeed the apple trees were still in bloom, the sky was blue and we were sitting on the ground by the edge of the orchard, looking over the farm and the big house. But neither of us thought of a ring and the only thing I could feel was a sharp sense of inevitability.

Edgar said something like, 'I guess this is it; what do you think?' And I said, 'yes, I think so…' and then, choosing my words carefully, said what had been on my mind for some time, that if we were to be married and if our marriage was to survive, we would have to have a space that was entirely our own. Nothing less would do. The house was fine (and I was ready to come out and live in this God-forsaken place), but I could not and would not share my life with his parents. I would not share the kitchen or any other room with his mother. We would have to live in completely separate quarters.

This was when Edgar showed his mettle, he is a man of action; and within three months, by the time we returned from our honeymoon, the upper floor was fixed as a handsome apartment with a spacious kitchen, a bathroom, a bedroom and a den.

The farm was small by Canadian standards (a 'hobby' farm of 20 acres), hidden away among giant tobacco and apple farms. One reached it by a paved rural road that also led to the municipal dump, a mile away. In the yard stood an old barn and a ramshackle garage that housed the two tractors and the spraying machine. At one time they had a cow and some pigs, but now there were only a few roaming chickens, some rabbits, a barn cat and two border collies.

The house had been built on a slight rise; to the east, in the gully, was the potato field; the apple orchard marched to the north; to the west lay Anna's vegetable garden and beyond ran a dirt road that marked the boundary of the property. All around lay tobacco fields, the bush, and more farmland. The nearest town was 20 km away. It took us an hour-and-a-half to drive to latihan (which we did diligently twice a week), and of course there was no public transport. (My darling aunt inquired in a letter if we had a light plane to get about...as in Australia...Well, no, dear...only a pick-up truck and a Mazda.) Edgar worked as a plant engineer in a town an hour away, and did whatever necessary on the farm in his after-hours. Few neighbours came by, only men and strictly on business. At times the only sounds to be heard were the staccato cries of the crows circling over the wood, and in the evening the haunting song of the Whip-poor-will.

A month after our wedding I received a letter from my mother's cousin, Dr. Anda Rudnizka. After congratulating me she added, '...I couldn't believe my eyes seeing the name Waniuk on the envelope. Did you know that it is a Belorussian name, and as common as Smith or Cohen? And did you know that the Belorussian were among the worst anti-Semites?' Then she went on to give me a short history of Belarus and its relationship to its neighbours the Ukraine and Poland, how for centuries it had been an underdog, always under foreign rule, presently under Russia. She ended the letter expressing hope that our union would be a bridge between our people. Amen, I thought, recalling my first encounter with Teodor. And I never told Anda, she would have been appalled, of the deep gulf that existed between our families; how the worlds Edgar and I came from were diametrically opposed: Russian Orthodox, illiterate peasantry on the one hand, Jewish, intellectual middle class on the other (though it was ironic that our families shared the same fate of displacement).

Illiteracy was for Teodor and Anna an insurmountable, even tragic, handicap. It isolated them from the society among which they lived, and held them prisoners in their own language, in each other's company, in their lost past and in their appalling ignorance.

Anna, in one of our better moments of communication, told me by way of excusing her illiteracy, that she had indeed been to school and had been a good scholar, but that in grade two they were obliged to learn a new alphabet. (Did the political situation then force the schools to replace the Latin alphabet with Cyrillic or vice versa?) Teodor the lazy, said Anna, played hooky, but she too stayed only for one more year, after which she was needed to look after the cows. She said that later, in the refugee camp in Africa, they were offered English classes, but that she was too busy working in the fields and looking after the children, and that Teodor, as usual, played cards.

It was virtually impossible to make music or paint while living with Edgar's parents. They didn't understand it and I could sense their mounting hostility. It was therefore the weaving that saved me – a creative activity that kept me going and kept me sane. It even served as a link of sorts with Anna who would come upstairs occasionally to watch me work, grudgingly appreciative. After all, she too had done much weaving in the Old Country. They did everything in the village by themselves, she said; all the women working together spinning and dyeing, weaving and felting. They made fabrics for bed sheets and garments, coats and blankets; they even made their own felted winter boots. Weaving was real work; she could understand that. But why bother now when one can get everything in the store?

These were small highlights, tentative points of contact, but they were short-lived. One day I invited her upstairs to help me with a knotted rug I was working on. It was only an excuse; the snow lay deep on the ground, she had nothing to do all day but sit in the kitchen and quarrel with Teodor and I thought to give her a break. She had to sit beside me and arrange on a tray small bundles of pre-cut wool; it helped speed up the knotting process. She came twice and seemed to enjoy herself. She talked incessantly (in her minimal English mixed with Polish), telling about their horrendous ordeals, about her life in the village, about her childhood... And then she stopped coming and evaded me elsewhere in the house. I didn't know what happened but eventually dragged the truth out from a very embarrassed Edgar: she had accused me of exploiting her.

I was hurt; but then what did I expect? These people had had a very difficult life; they were survivors and that was the only thing that mattered. Also I had to allow that Anna would never accept me: I was a stranger who had 'taken' her son away from her. Thus I listened daily to their angry voices, rising like poisonous arrows from their kitchen to mine. Why wasn't I younger, why didn't I work in the fields, why didn't Paul marry a strong Russian girl who would bear him many children?

There was nothing I could do but follow my latihan. And in repeated testing I was guided to remain uninvolved, stay away, and ignore.

In Jerusalem, in the first year of having received the 'gift', I did a series of six coloured drawings, each representing a recognizable landscape: a pristine beach in early morning; an aerial view of the coastline; sunset and sunrise in the desert; a beautiful meadow I had seen in a dream; and one that depicted a wet field bordered by cedars, with a bit of brown earth, a hint of a distant forest, and a gray misty sky. Altogether a foreign place I didn't know. Yet whenever I looked at it, my eyes would fill with tears; and I kept wondering what kind of place it was, if it was from the future, and why the tears?

The drawing had been long forgotten when on one of my walks I came across it at the border of our neighbour's cornfield. There it was:

the slanting green field, the cedars, the sandpit and the distant wood. And what's more, that inexplicable sadness was present too; a heavy melancholy that lay like a pall over the land – though, mind you, not on that cornfield but only on our property, from border to border.

Once I even tested it, walking along the dirt road stepping off onto the neighbour's tobacco field, then onto our orchard, receiving, respectively, neutrality and heaviness. I was quite aware that this oppression could have been merely a projection of my negativity. But instinctively I mostly stayed indoors and took my daily walks – later pushing the baby stroller – away from the farm. And yet there are a few stories that retain a certain 'gothic' flavour that leaves the question open and unanswered.

There is the story about Shep, the Border collie. Shep and Blackie were handsome dogs, but shy. They avoided all my overtures and were loyal to Teodor only. One day I noticed that Shep, who was the larger, more intelligent and spirited of the two, was limping. It was a piece of glass that had got embedded in his paw, which I removed with Edgar's help. From that moment on Shep became my best friend, greeting me with great exuberance whenever I stepped out of the house. It felt simply wonderful. I had made my first conquest and had finally a dog as an ally in that wretched place. But that honeymoon was short lived, for ten days later Shep got himself killed, run over while chasing the neighbour's truck. It was a freakish accident and the neighbour felt awful, but I couldn't shake off the feeling that I should have left Shep alone; that it happened because of me; that something in this place resented goodwill and friendship of any kind.

I never stayed out after dark (too many mosquitoes). But once – that was already after the parents had gone to live in a senior home – I remained puttering in the vegetable garden till dusk, when I became aware of a creepy, cold and clammy sensation that was hovering about me, so that my hair stood on end. Something was out there, in the deepening shadows in the direction of the gaping foundations – something that was malevolent. I wasn't given time to 'investigate' for directly I received an urgent inner command; 'Get into the house at once!' and I was pushed unceremoniously from behind, my legs barely able to catch up, back to the safety of the house.

And then there was the gnarled, old apple tree that harboured in its hollow trunk a large colony of hornets; and it was evil. One could easily sense the threat that emanated from it, and it wasn't because of the hornets only – that, you might say, was a tangible, 'good' threat – the other felt different, eerie, sinister and very old. One day Edgar took it into his head to prune the tree. It was useless to dissuade him, so I stood by the window and watched. One moment he was standing safely among the branches sawing away, and the next he was flying, to hit the ground with a sickening thud, flat on his back. I could have sworn the tree had pushed him off, literally! Edgar wasn't hurt, only stunned. In all the years he had been pruning trees he had never experienced anything like it. But only when little Linda, an inquisitive three-year old visitor, stuck her hand into the hollow and was attacked by the hornets, did Edgar resolve to burn the tree down; it smouldered for weeks.

I didn't tell Edgar or anyone else about my 'observations'. But then Michael Greenstein, a Subud member from London, came by one day on some business. He was the 'macho' type, notorious for his acerbic tongue, yet when he stepped out of the car his first words to me were: 'how can you stand it here?'

'Why? What?'

'This heaviness; the moment I left the paved road to enter the farm it hit my chest like a ton of bricks; I could hardly breathe!'

So this whole thing was not simply a figment of my imagination!

Once, on one of our long drives to latihan, I had a receiving that we would stay on the farm not longer than five years. Perhaps that was why I didn't pester Edgar to leave the place sooner. And indeed things began to change of their own accord so that we were out of there by the spring of 1983.

Yet I consider that time on the farm as one of the most difficult periods of my life. In my letters to Israel I likened it to living on a submarine; confined, isolated, uneasy, guarded – I was in enemy territory. No doubt it was also an extraordinary rich and rewarding time, what with the coming of our daughter, the deepening ties with my husband, and my personal growth. But if it hadn't been for the latihan and all those dreams and signs to guide me, I would not have dared go where angels fear to tread, and would not have gone through with this marriage.

In the summer before the wedding, troubled and questioning my decision, I retreated for the duration of the Ramadan to be on my own. I had a dream.

A man resembling both Ze'ev and Edgar arrives at my house on a bicycle, wearing a shiny green silk suit – the brightest green of early spring; while I, waiting for him on the porch, have on a long evening dress of raw silk in a silvery green colour – the colour of autumn grasses.

I understood the dream to be confirmation that my step was the right one and that this was the man I should marry. We are both in green silk – the colour here symbolizing worship but also indicating that this would be a union of harmonizing opposites.

Anna

An inexplicable heaviness has dogged me all morning! I plunk down in front of the computer, barely able to sit up. And that's when I notice the date; today is the eighth of July and a quick calculation tells me that it is the eighth anniversary of Anna's death. That would explain it: today is 'Anna's day'... And once again I marvel how everything comes together, since this is where I am at, toiling on the umpteenth revision of this story, grappling with the relentless pull of its emotional vortex, unable to hold my head above water.

Now, all of a sudden, I can see my way out.

During the first two years on the farm, while living with Edgar's parents, I thought it was because of Teodor that I felt so threatened, since it was he who visibly appalled and repelled me. With Anna, at least, I could talk a little, but with Teodor there was no communication, not a shred of understanding, and no acknowledgment. Yet now I see that his was only the threat of a harmless, cornered animal – irrational, emotional, and directed against the world at large; against everything and everyone, but not necessarily towards me personally.

On the other hand, the one who truly mattered was Anna; it had always been about her!

Granted, Anna was the proverbial mother-in-law and I had to endure her open and veiled criticism, her foolish rivalry, and her hostility; yet at the core of our antagonism was something bigger; it was about a clash of worlds, in which, improbable as it may sound, she had the upper hand. For Anna believed herself superior to everyone she knew – excepting her son, that is, who was the apple of her eye – and regarded me, in particular, as ineffectual and useless. The absurdity was that I cared! Her power was such that she couldn't be dismissed and I had a devil of a time to ignore and forget – as those repeated testings indicated I should.

And this is what I understood today; that it wasn't my story that mattered but Anna's; and that by telling it – even if only in the sketchiest way – I shall win half the battle. At least it will bring about a certain understanding, which in itself is an antidote for enmity.

It was impossible to make sense of what had happened. Edgar didn't help either. He seldom translated what was being said and, in the typical fashion of a son who is impatient with his parents, he washed his hands of their past, his own included – Edgar has no past. Thus it has taken me years to fit all the bits of information I gleaned from Anna's jumbled stories into a historical context.

Teodor Waniuk (1899–1990) and Anna née Kuzmicz (1902–1997) lived in a village near Luninec in the southwestern region of Belarus (which since 1919 had been a Polish territory). Anna was the youngest in her family and, as far as I could make out, the only daughter. She said that her five brothers were all giants, as was her father, and that they used to joke good-naturedly about her being so small.

Of Teodor I know only that he came from a nearby village, that he had been married before, and had a son, Walter, from his first marriage.

World War II began on September 1st 1939, when Germany invaded Poland from the west. On September 17, Stalin, who had signed a pact with Hitler to divide Poland between them, invaded Poland from the east. Eastern Poland was annexed to the Soviet Union, and a systematic cleansing of the 'socially dangerous anti-Soviet elements' began. On February 1940, Stalin decreed a mass deportation of the intelligentsia, the middle class, and the peasantry to Siberia. The Waniuks were among the deportees, swept like millions of others into this terrible tsunami of events.

But when was that horrendous train journey they talked about? Was it on the cattle trucks on the way to Siberia, or later on the long journey south? How did they fare in the labour camp? And the biggest mystery of all, how did they end up in a Polish refugee camp in Northern Rhodesia?

A chance article in a newspaper gave me the missing clue. For it is a little known fact that in June 1941, when Germany began its Operation Barbarossa, the surprise invasion of Russia, Stalin, in need of as many allies as he could get, opened the labour camps and released the Poles (ultimately to facilitate the creation of a Polish army). Almost a million people were let go. Thus began their second terrible journey – during which many froze to death, or perished from exhaustion, disease and starvation. Talking about this journey Anna and Teodor would get animated, calling out the names of the countries they had crossed, enumerating them on their fingers, reminding and correcting each other: Siberia, India, Pakistan, Afghanistan, also Turkey and Syria, and Iran.

Iran at that point became a safe haven for the hundreds of thousands of refugees that were streaming out of Russia. In due course, with the collaboration of the British and Polish Forces, a great number of these refugees, the Waniuks among them, were shipped from Iran to camps in British East Africa, to Tanganyika, now Zambia. There they stayed for the duration of the war, and there the children, Marie and Paul, were born. Anna told me that she didn't even know she was pregnant until well into her sixth month, she thought it was the menopause.

After the war, unable to return to Poland, the refugees were taken back to England, to yet another camp (near Stafford). Ten years later, in 1958, with the aid of Edgar's half-brother (who had served in the Polish army), the family immigrated to Canada and settled on a farm in Southern Ontario.

Their daughter Marie left home after high school to continue her education and start a new life for herself; and Edgar went on to study engineering, with the full support of his mother and against the wishes of his father, who wanted him to become a garage mechanic.

Anna was a fiercely self-reliant and resourceful woman; her small bent stature belying her physical strength and her determination. She had charisma and could still charm strangers with her sharp eye and seeming naiveté. But beneath it she was hard and calculating, self-centred and critical. In her extreme old age when we visited her in the senior home, she'd talk incessantly, with a monotonous drone, the little English she knew forgotten. Edgar would manage sometimes to interject a word, while Ilana and I would sit numb with tedium and wait for the visit to end. But sometimes she would become her old self, alert and competitive; then she'd acknowledge my presence by challenging me: 'Silvana, look!' She'd roll up her sleeves and show her arms and her still beautiful and clever hands, 'see, strong!' Then she'd bend down to touch her toes, 'see, I can! They,' – pointing to the general direction of the Home and describing in the air a corpulent body – 'no can!' And she'd chuckle triumphantly.

She liked to brag that it was only thanks to her that they survived. 'Not Teodor, Teodor nothing!' But she worked, always, in the fields in Turkey and Iran, in Africa and England and, of course, in Canada. Of one story she was particularly proud; how before the evacuation she cunningly wrapped sheets around her body, adding layers of clothing on top, which she later bartered for bread, thus she and Teodor 'eat' while 'many many die on the train …'

Faith played a central role in her life (not so for Teodor). She prayed daily; I have often seen her in an attitude of prayer. A few times a year, on their special holidays, Edgar would take her to church, which was a fair distance away. On Easter mornings she and Teodor would appear in our apartment, sprinkling holy water in all the rooms – 'Christ has risen.'

I didn't tell her I was Jewish – her daughter did. And then she was magnanimous. It was my first month on the farm, around Rosh Hashanah, and she surprised me by wishing me a happy New Year. 'It is your New Year, yes? I know!' And she told me about the rabbi in her village, how he was respected for his wide knowledge: 'he was a good man, he help many people.'

There is one image that pretty much sums her up for me. It was late spring and she had been working in her garden till after sunset. Now she entered the house, in her baggy pants, her hand-sewn, padded jacket, and her perennial woollen hat, and I saw that her face was covered with blood, bright-red rivulets streaming down her paper-white skin.

Horrified I called out: 'what happened?'

She waved me away. 'No, no, okay, okay! Flies, flies…'

Only the notorious blood-sucking black flies of early summer. This selfless dedication to her work impressed me immensely, even as I suspected an element of show: here she was working so hard so late, while her lazy, good-for-nothing husband was watching television and I, the city girl, had not a clue what real work was all about.

I sympathized with her. Teodor was such an unpleasant man, always angry, shouting, complaining or accusing. There she was, stuck with him for life in this isolated, lonely place. Much later it dawned on me that it wasn't Anna who was being abused; it wasn't she who was the victim; it was Teodor; he was the hen-pecked husband who could do nothing right by his wife. Teodor was the weak one and thus he vented his anger and frustrations on the world and, in particular, on his son, who, it seemed, could do nothing right by his father. But when asked about his father, Edgar gave me a warning look not to ask further questions saying, 'he is not a very nice man.'

But what was it about Teodor anyway? He didn't drink, and he was not violent. It was only this permanent black cloud that hung over him that was so appalling. Not able to understand or communicate, and being overly sensitive to his irate voice, I nevertheless wanted to seek out his better side, uncover some hidden goodness beneath his disagreeable exterior. I still can see him in a moment of solitude, standing in the yard under the locust tree, looking over the rolling land, the potato field, the distant bush; his face inscrutable beneath his khaki hat. Absentmindedly he fishes out of his pocket a can of tobacco and slowly rolls himself a cigarette, while Blackie crouches beside him, watching, waiting, tense, quivering. Then the man stirs and starts to stride towards the fields and the dog, released, shoots like an arrow, gliding over the land, his tail streaming out behind him, disappearing in the distance, coming back, circling the man and shooting off again. A man and his dog alone and at peace.

In the winter in early 1980, Teodor, who had turned 81, became agitated and disturbed. It began when Edgar, to improve the orchard, hired experienced men to prune the trees – a yearly time-consuming job. Teodor, however, insisting on his own old method, and unwilling to accept theirs, became uncharacteristically violent and, wielding a pitchfork like a mad man, chased the workers off the property. The situation was getting out of hand and we consulted the family doctor and a social worker. Apparently Teodor was very healthy but old age was catching up with him. It would be best, they advised, for his general state of mind, if he could get away from the farm and its responsibilities. Had we ever considered moving the parents to a senior home?

No, Edgar had never considered this option though I secretly did. For Edgar, this had been a simple matter: it was his duty to care for his parents and there was nothing more to be said. But now that the situation was changing, he embraced the new idea in his usual positive, matter-of-fact way. After some searching we found an excellent place, The Ivan Franco Home, a Ukrainian establishment, in Mississauga. There they would be amidst people whose language they understood, and amidst a culture they could relate to. Their names were put on the waiting list and sooner than expected a vacancy opened, and they moved in that same summer, two months after the birth of Ilana.

Anna surprised me when she said she had been waiting a long time to get away, and that she didn't want to work outside or cook for Teodor anymore. When she left the house for the last time, wearing one of her seldom worn better dresses, she hobbled resolutely towards the car, never looking back. But Teodor took his time gazing over the farm, tears running down his worn cheeks.

Post Script

Canada was in a deep recession in 1982, yet Edgar, who had been looking around for some time, received an excellent job offer from Ralston Purina in Mississauga, where he started working that same winter. However selling the farm proved more difficult; the house was, after all, rather a 'white elephant'. It was May 1983 when we finally moved to Mississauga. Standing at the window of our modest, new, suburban home, looking over a monotonous sea of subdivisions I was elated; this was a most wonderful sight! No more will I look over desolate snow covered fields; no more shall I listen to the mournful call of the whip-poor-will; I was back in the folds of civilization…

Teodor and Anna adjusted to their new life in Ivan Franco and, as predicted, once away from the cares of the farm, Teodor began to relax. His face opened up, the angry lines smoothed away and it was apparent that a great burden had been taken off his shoulders. But the most astonishing change was his burgeoning love for our baby daughter! The tenderness that shone from his eyes as he held her in his arms was a sight to behold. Teodor, as it turned out, was a softie at heart. He also cried when the nine-year-old Ilana played for him on her violin. But Anna, at this stage of her life, seemed to have lost the ability to show affection. Oh yes, she would remember fondly how clever her little Pawel was at the age of two, but she could not relate to her grandchildren.

I believe that Teodor was proof, as Bapak had explained, that when we do the latihan we also help our parents and ancestors – sons help the male line of their family, daughters the female. It was quite evident that Edgar's latihan had a direct effect on his father. Teodor had become a changed man.

For his 90th birthday we gave him a little party in our home. He was shy and beamed like a happy boy. When, if ever, had his birthday been celebrated? (Anna, on that occasion, was peevish and behaved like a jealous sibling.)

Another time I had to take Teodor to the hospital, to the day clinic, for some minor treatment. The staff spoke Polish. They noticed that it was his 91st birthday and made a great fuss over him. Teodor rose to the occasion; he flirted with the nurses, exchanged jokes with the chiropodist, and when we left did a happy shuffle dance along the corridor. I watched with amazement.

He died 7 months later, very peacefully. He had just gone to have a nap after lunch…

Anna outlived him by seven years. She gloated that she had fought with death and won. Yet towards the end, her life was a senseless existence without grace. In her last battle she was taken to the hospital with respiratory problems where for weeks she continued to fight, holding onto life. The priest had come and bestowed the last rites; Edgar visited regularly, as did his sister; but I received to stay away.

Then one Sunday I knew I should come along – that this was the day. When we entered I saw that the other bed was vacant and that Anna had the room to herself. The coast was clear and it was time that I did a latihan for her. She needed help to let go and be ready for her next journey.

She was hooked to machines and was asleep or unconscious. I hardly recognized her. Always small, she was now tiny like a dying sparrow, just a small heap of skin and bones; there was nothing left but her grim determination to stay alive. Edgar stood sentinel outside while I began the latihan; it was a very quiet latihan, just standing by her bed and singing softly, like a lullaby; it didn't last long. Her face relaxed in her sleep, the tight, pinched lines seemed gentler and she murmured something with the trace of a smile as if she was a child again talking to her mother... When Edgar entered she seemed to be awake and to recognize him. He bent over, kissed her forehead and bid her goodbye. She died that night towards dawn.

The night following her grandmother's funeral, Ilana, who had just turned seventeen, received a spontaneous latihan; it was her first. An official opening was conducted three months later.

PART FIVE
A SUBUD CRISIS

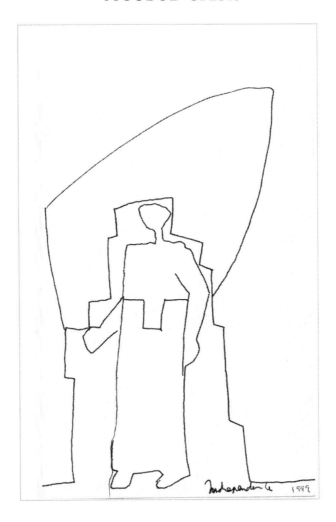

World Subud Council Meeting, 1987

My appointment to the job of international helper (IH) was a low-key affair. There was none of the pomp and circumstance that dominated the testing for the IHs that Bapak did, in front of all and sundry, at the congress of 1983.

It was September 1986 when Lorraine Mason, an IH for Area III (the Americas), called me from Portland, Oregon. One of the IHs had resigned; they were looking for a replacement and compiling a list of candidates to send to Bapak. Would I be willing to have my name put forward? Breathless – I couldn't say 'I don't know, let me think it over' – I said 'yes'.

Afterwards I remembered the experience I had had the previous week that, in all likelihood, was a kind of preparation for this call and for what was to come. I was on my way to pick up Ilana from school, walking briskly down the street, when I felt a sudden change of awareness, from the everyday to an extraordinary sense of peace, combined with a broadening of my consciousness, which expanded and grew in widening circles like a radar, to reach far beyond the present, beyond this place and this country, to embrace the whole world! It lasted probably only a split second, but I knew that this was the sort of awareness an international helper should have, ideally, and that in two years' time, when my term as national helper was over, I could be ready for the job! I had never thought about it, I didn't believe I had the capacity, but now it seemed a possibility.

Lorraine phoned back six weeks later (by then I had forgotten the whole thing) to inform me that Bapak had approved my name.

For the first six months on the 'job' I was in a kind of limbo and did almost nothing; it was frustrating and discouraging. The job makes sense only when the helpers work together as a team or *dewan*. But the international helpers are few and far between, and with little available money to cover travelling costs, the helpers (3 from Chile, 2 from the United States, and I from Canada) had difficulties meeting even once a year (though I did travel to Portland to meet with my American counterparts). The Internet was still in its embryonic stages and although I was supplied with an electronic-mail device, the experts I summoned didn't have a clue how to make it work. But even after I was finally initiated into its mysteries, I thought the machine a very poor substitute for human contact.

Thus my job proper began in the summer of 1987 when I went to Indonesia to attend the World Subud Council (WSC) meeting at Wisma Subud, Cilandak, Jakarta, which coincided with the *Selamatan* for the fortieth day of the passing away of Bapak.

As expected this was a particularly challenging time. The WSC had to prepare the groundwork for the upcoming world congress in Sydney, the first without Bapak, and had to assume new initiatives and responsibilities amidst discord and chaos, amidst unrealistic expectations and while emotions were flying high. Bereft of Bapak's wisdom and leadership, the going was rough. But everyone did his or her best, and by the grace of God we pulled through.

I was the new kid on the block in more than one sense. Not only had these people been working together now for three years, but many of them were also veterans in Subud who had met Bapak personally and had served the brotherhood, as it were, from day one. I came on board through the back door and needed chutzpah (a quality which apparently I had) to speak up in such a milieu. Though, and I say it with wonder, there were a few instances when it wasn't my chutzpah but a higher power that spoke through me; truly a most peculiar feeling – not unlike what Balaam's ass might have felt when 'the Lord opened the mouth of the donkey' (Numbers XXII, 28).

It is said that when you take on a job in Subud, you will be given the strength to do it. And indeed I was very much aware that I was functioning on borrowed strength, on a temporary mandate, riding on a mix of energy, of which the greater part was not mine. To 'come down' from such heights was a great relief; for the job is very heavy. But I believe that I was also rewarded generously afterwards. Still in a subtle way, for better or for worse, the job has marked me for life.

The following notes are excerpts from a diary I kept during the 1987 World Subud Council meeting. It was my first attempt to write a diary in English and the only one I wrote during my term as IH. As it is not an historical document but a personal account of an extraordinary time, I omitted whatever I deemed too personal, irrelevant, or obsolete, and stories of others that are not for me to tell. Also I have chosen to tamper as little as possible with my original English, for fear it would take away from its immediacy.

July 30th

I arrived at Wisma Subud at 5:00 pm. (Met R. in the airport and we took a taxi together.) People keep arriving, tired, with swollen feet, jetlagged. It is a great feeling to meet old and new faces.

There is going to be a reading from the Koran and Susila Budhi Dharma at Bapak's house in Pamulang. This is the last night before the 40th day Selamatan. So I brave it, as do many other weary travellers. It is a long and bumpy drive through endless makeshift neighbourhoods, and congested traffic. Pamulang is an oasis (for the rich). The pendopo [a free standing open structure that serves as auditorium] in front of Bapak's new house is most impressive.

July 31st

Morning – informal helpers meeting; from a trickle of three to almost the whole dewan. As I am writing this a day later and as yesterday has slipped back into the dawn of history, I don't remember a thing.

Afternoon – we 'the privileged' travelled in air-conditioned buses to the Selamatan. The driveway to Bapak's house was lit with hundreds of candles and looked very festive. Many cars and buses arrived. There must have been close to thousand people and many had to sit outside the pendopo. I sat close to the centre so as not to miss a thing. But I was disappointed, for the event turned out to be a purely traditional Muslim ceremony with prayers from the Koran and endless repetitions of 'Allah'hu Akbar'...

Anyway I tried to remain alert and in touch with my inner and with Bapak, whose presence I had felt so clearly last month; and thus I was repeatedly made to watch Mas Adji, Bapak's grandson. I'd sit quietly watching the imams and my head would turn sharply to the left, to fix my eyes on him. This happened a few times – so I permitted myself to observe him. I saw his tremendous sorrow and his deep love for Bapak but I also perceived his nature, his strength and weakness, the great capacity of his heart and emotions, the beauty of it and the danger...How people could easily get carried away and be drawn to him like flies to honey. (Later, back in my room, I had a hard time to shake off these feelings.)

After the prayers each of the guests were offered a gift-box filled with Javanese delicacies and a special present: the new book of Bapak's last days – *Remembrances*. There were not enough copies to go round, and one little old Indonesian lady was so disappointed that I gave her mine. (Afterwards I could kick myself. There you are – false charity.)

August 1st

Early latihan, then meeting with trustees [zonal representatives]. The initial purpose from the helpers' point of view was to facilitate a dialogue and bring about better bonding through the ironing out of personal and general aspects relating to their job. It turned out differently. Varindra Vittachi [chair of the WSC], who presided over the meeting, gave a very moving talk, after which it became a mutual exchange of what people were expecting from this meeting... Basically it was helpers versus the organization concerning the lack of funds. It was harmonious but unsatisfactory. So we met again in the evening. And once again while the helpers were trying to guide (gently) towards testing sessions the trustees, clearly not interested, were for their part busy formulating their ideas and concerns about Subud. A long evening! We'll meet again tomorrow.

In the afternoon the helpers met to test two questions: 1) the present state of the Subud brotherhood and the direction it should take; and 2) how each of us can contribute to the spread of the latihan and the growth of Subud.

Generally we received for 1) that the brotherhood is oscillating and dragging its feet in a state of confusion, and though the vision is there, there is no clear way towards it. But guidance and direction will come through a new awareness of the latihan and the worship of God, and from that the strength and growth.

2) Concerning my contribution to the growth of Subud: I had a powerful experience that took me to another plane – new to me. I was not on the ground but in a rarefied place reaching down, as if through clouds… Afterwards I was in an emotional state and questioned if that meant that I was going to die soon. But I didn't say much about it or about the reaching down business. More specific details emerged from what my sisters received for me. My strong points, according to them, are my capacity of awareness, of being able to have an overview of a situation, personal strength and charm, and reaching people through my roots.

Testing for my sisters showed most movingly, how unique and diverse are the manifestations of surrender and worship in each of us.

August 2nd

Slept only 3 hours; was woken up at 4:00 a.m. and that was that.

9:00 a.m. – latihan.

10:00 a.m. – meeting of trustees and IHs, to continue the meeting from the previous day…We agreed to separate. Each party has its own work to do, and 'mixing' isn't healthy for the smooth operation of either.

Afternoon partially free – a rare opportunity for the helpers from Area III to meet and deal with issues relating to their own Area…

A party was forming on the guesthouse veranda: coffee and cakes… many visitors….Socializing…Talked with Y. who had lived here for many years. The reason for the rigid Muslim ceremony, she explained, is for protection against fanaticism; the lack of Subud content in the ceremony, which I lamented, would have been provided, on other occasions, by Bapak ...

8:00 p.m. – The official opening ceremony. Bapak's family was all present. There were speeches by Varindra, by some of the IHs, and others...Then Bapak's son, Mas Harjono, spoke. He began by telling us about the questions reporters had been putting to Bapak's family, regarding who was going to succeed Bapak, and the family's unanimous, though unplanned, reply that there is no one to succeed him 'as such'. He told about the position of Subud in Indonesia: small in numbers but strong in structure, in performance, and in public opinion...He placed Bapak's family as part of the Subud structure. Bapak's family is a fact, biological and historical and has to be reckoned with. He expressed his thanks to Ibu Rahayu [Bapak's eldest daughter] that she is willing to be of help, but stressed that it was only as an advisor. He finished by urging us to cherish this new sense of strength and inner connection to Bapak and to God that so many had been experiencing, and to remember love and kindness in our dealings.

August 4th

This is yesterday's report.

Latihan – after some confusion with latihan space (there are always those who get hurt so easily; what do the people expect of each other? We are not saints! It's time to be more courteous and polite and not take each other for granted...)

First plenary session – I think I'll skip that one; too many emotions.

Afternoon – Work parties. Helpers to deal with some of the immediate issues raised by the Brotherhood and Ibu Rahayu (i.e. who should sign helpers' cards? How will the international helpers be chosen? Who will give names?)

I am ashamed to say that we acted like an unruly crowd and not like a dewan: jumpy, heady, telling each other off. We did try a few times to 'sit quiet' but it was lip service; the quiet never materialized. I suggested that we appoint one of us to chair the meeting. R was quick to volunteer – and unfortunately he 'took over', constantly intervening and interjecting; but at least we could begin to do some work.

Early this morning H. took me to Bapak's grave. This was very beneficial and a great help to find some balance after the complete collapse of last evening. Entering the Jakarta cemetery was quite disturbing, but to enter the family enclosure was to enter peace. Bapak's grave is still without a headstone and is covered with flowers. I was compelled to kneel and be very empty. Later I prayed, asking God for help, for courage, and patience – especially regarding the latest happenings. I sat quietly and listened to my inner feeling slowly calming down, surrendering everything, also the wish to set things right. Then I heard Bapak's voice within me, 'Finis!' And that was all. Now it is up to me to keep this peace.

At ten in the morning the IHs met with Ibu Rahayu. What a lovely lady, wise and unassuming; also very practical, attentive, and flexible. We the IHs appeared to be divided into three groups: the ones that didn't say a word; those who constantly interfered, interpreted, explained, and generally were becoming a nuisance; and those who had a 'big mouth' and asked questions. Well...when I thought again to explode, the quiet ones became more assertive, the 'interpreters' slowed down, and Me and Co. shut our mouth a bit, and the meeting ended very well.

Now the next job is to deal with the snowball that started last night: a) Varindra's vision to set up a Foundation under the name of Bapak – the Muhammad Subuh Foundation, and b) the buying of Bapak's old house. [An idea which had been put forward by a group of American entrepreneurs regarding the Big House at Wisma Subud, which the family had recently put on the market]. Trustees are dissatisfied at the pace of events, the feelings attached to it, and the way it is handled.

At midnight, after an awfully sleepy general meeting, we met with the trustees only, to discuss the latest development. Generally we established a feeling of openness and a common ground...Though even that late at night, within all that quiet, some of us were not able to stay within their peace and were 'out of tune'...All in all we weren't too bad; we really did our best and God knows it.

In bed at two… This night I slept like a log for four whole hours! What luxury! By the way it was the holiest of the Muslim holidays, Abraham's sacrifice of Ishmael, and the chanting and praying from the surrounding mosques engulfed the world with an amazing din for 12 solid hours, from sunset to sunrise. My earplugs were a necessity and did the trick. This was the first night since the meeting began that I slept soundly and for so long.

August 5th

The morning session was one good reason for the deep sleep. After consulting with Ibu Rahayu, Varindra announced that she and the family would not give their consent to having Bapak's name used in connection with any kind of Foundation or whatever, as our possible wrong actions could drag Bapak's name into the dirt…So Varindra – tearful and a bit shaken surrendered the whole idea [for the time being].

Afternoon: long meeting with Wilbert Verheyen, the Chair of Susila Dharma International – the charitable arm of Subud. He called the meeting to urge the IHs to remember SDI in their visits to the groups.

Then a meeting with the Budget working party: endless back and forth about how to fund the IHs travels. Then our own Area III helpers meeting; hashing old stuff. Then time for the BBQ.

9:00 p.m. – latihan and testing with X…

10:00 p.m. – meeting at the Big House. Present: Varindra, the trustees, the IHs, and the team that is working on the proposal to have the house purchased by the brotherhood. The presentation was tiring and one-sided and it became clear to me (and to Varindra who watched me with a mischievous glint in his eye) that I was out of my depth; so by eleven I called it a day, and left.

August 6th

Another short night: I am wide-awake since quarter to five and thinking about this latest hurdle. My absolute gut feeling is NO! This is not the time to appeal to the brotherhood for more funds! There is a core of people who would like to preserve the house for its historical and emotional value – it has been Bapak's home for twenty years, but the fact is that the house is empty; there is nothing there! For me and I can fairly assume for a considerable part of the brotherhood that had never been to Cilandak and had never met Bapak, this place has no particular meaning... I cannot give my support to such an approach... Also I cannot see this particular house or any house becoming a kind of shrine or, as someone said, 'a museum for our children...a place to learn about Subud...'

The general meeting went well until the subject of the Big House came up. Emotions flared up, and with such conflicting points of view there wasn't a chance to pass a resolution; things will have to calm down and be re-evaluated.

Meanwhile Varindra had to leave for personal reasons...

We, the women helpers had a good meeting; I was frustrated at the impasse, but calm talking and sharing restored everybody's balance. When we met with the men, R. pointed out that we have not been performing our duty as helpers and had in many ways been interfering in the work of the committee.

Everyone is totally spent, so we took the evening off, just socializing in the Big House; a little wasteful, considering our time limit, but probably necessary.

August 7th

Passed the evening with Lorraine, M. and L.; good sharing. Lorraine needed some of that because her cup was full to the brim and overflowing. We are getting there one by one. Yesterday it was M. who all but threw in the towel. K. is sitting on a barrel of dynamite; I may have reached that point yesterday or maybe the worst is yet to come. R. H. is flat on his back; F. and T. are choked with tears; R. T. is hanging in there but he is leaving in 2 days...Two days! With what we are going through here it is like eternity! We are trying to work together; but how can 18 people [the IHs], wonderful individuals each and everyone accomplish it without a chairperson, a secretary, an agenda or a protocol? And we had never had the time to stop and figure it out...

We did cover more ground today and were productive, until the devil stuck his foot in the door. Guess who? M. [one of the trustees]! Please forgive me God. He is a super guy but I don't trust him; and he this afternoon 'innocently' pushed a draft of resolution into R.'s hands, for the helpers to 'comment' on; fair enough, yes? NO!

We wasted again two hours doing committee work; examining this paper, arguing on its text, content and procedure, fighting, getting angry; in short devil got his way almost too easily, the more so since R. was his instrument; R. who spent all morning formulating a modus operandi of interaction with the trustees (how much we interfere, when, etc.). And this good brother just had his lesson when he realized (the same moment I did) what we were doing; giving support to *one* trustee and his draft of resolution. I am speechless!

August 8th

I can hardly believe that only one week has passed since the beginning of this meeting. It seems like a thousand days. Ten more before I go home...I'll need a lot of patience.

Today was the formal closing ceremony in Pamulang. So off we went, in air-conditioned mini buses. This time it was by day so one could see the countryside; well not exactly. The city is sprawling ever outwards, filth and red dust and garbage everywhere, but also there are some more well-to-do suburbs, banana plantations, and rice fields.

A lovely setup awaited us under the pendopo and the atmosphere was formal and festive. Ian Arnold, the ISC [International Subud Committee] vice-chair, addressed council with an honest and probing speech after which all the trustees spoke in turn and then some of the international helpers. I found the courage to speak too. I have been talking so much these days, and doing so much writing, that after a shaky start I calmed down and aware of my inner guidance I said what I wanted to say. This was a very special exercise and I thanked God in wonder. I will not be surprised to find that all this 'inflated me' will shrivel up and disappear once I am on the plane...

August 9th

The concert last night was a very nice Subud event; 'Quality A' as R. said. My contribution was 4 short duets played with a visiting member from Christchurch, N.Z. We rehearsed for only half an hour before the concert on two guitars borrowed from the International

School. During our performance I experienced again this special gift from the morning; an inner clarity to overcome any obstacles of fear and confusion; we played well.

This morning an Area III meeting to identify and clarify a variety of subjects: communication, Zonal Gatherings, our functions as IHs... Good meeting though I had moments of total absence. Strange; I was brought back only by immersing myself in the mirror image of sky and trees on the glass surface of the coffee table. The immediate reality was too difficult. The peace within that sky in the glass restored me. I don't know why, but tears came to my eyes, which alarmed my colleagues; did they say something wrong? Well, by then I was okay...

August 10th

Last night I had to retire early. A great weakness overtook me, especially in the stomach. I couldn't even brush my teeth. I lay on the bed unable to lift my head or move. I slept till shortly after four but though awake the weakness was still paralyzing. The energy I had been given for the last ten days was now totally spent. I was left like an abandoned useless thing. Void. Nothing in me stirs. I am motionless. Then I hear a door slam; Edgar is going to work ...but of course I am in Wisma Subud! Still this brought me back. There is an everyday simple reality awaiting me when I come home. It's okay. Today I'll go shopping – yes! Hold on to something ordinary; be 'normal'.

Everybody is wiped out and we have changed. Our 'mission complete', something is withdrawing. The force of wanting to unite is retreating; everyone is going somewhere – putting an invisible barrier between themselves and the rest. The parting process is working and the sadness is very eloquent.

But my strength is coming back. I am able to write and face the day. The extra week here will help me to return to a normal state, I hope, so that I won't have to burden my family when I come home – a week of transition.

Yesterday in the afternoon another helpers meeting in the garden; the group is getting smaller and it is therefore easier to move on. We managed to do some more business when M. came forward, expressing his disappointment about the lack of spiritual content in our meetings, and K. joined in adding her frustration that she was not asked to share her first hand experience of Bapak's last day with us. The suggestion to separate for latihan and testing was continually sabotaged by those who had to say the last word, or others who had to straighten the record… Again I had the courage to let myself get into a 'tantrum'. As I have made a name for myself for being emotional and impulsive, I felt I could do it again, for the sake of the afternoon and our harmony. My tantrum worked and soon we separated; the men to do latihan and testing; and we, as we had already done latihan earlier, just sat quietly together in the failing light and let K slowly unfold her story. Then we all in turn told ours and shared another rare moment of sisterly intimacy and bonding.

The day is not over yet. After breakfast I collapsed on the bed once again and was gone for another two hours, not able to move or open my eyes. I thought I'd stay like that forever. A dream brought me back. It was about Ilana. I neglected her. She was with other people, dressed poorly, almost naked, and emotionally lost – a sad and disturbing dream. I have now to go home and care for her; I did my job for a while…others will continue… And as we are all only pawns in the Big Game I am not going to let myself feel inadequate; I have been shown my value and my part in it….

The Bird

The year 1994 was another watershed of sorts. A momentous change was brewing, of which I first became aware during the national congress that took place north of Toronto, on Victoria Day. This was the last event of its kind I would attend for many years to come.

I had arrived armed with some insights I wanted to share with the helpers. But everyone seemed strangely unconcerned and indifferent, and when a helpers meeting did finally materialize and I got my chance to speak, no one listened or cared; in fact I was rudely ignored. It wasn't personal – only, like in a dream, I felt disoriented. Something was up! Perhaps it was time that I bowed out and went home.

For the remainder of the day I facilitated, with Ilana's help, an art workshop. We set it up in a remote room and worked peacefully with cardboard, x-acto knives, glue and paint. Kids and adults dropped in to make masks, which were later exhibited in the common room.

As we drove home that night, a gigantic full moon shone in the east, and in the north fireworks lit up the sky over Canada's Wonderland. We arrived after midnight. Edgar and Ilana soon retired, but I took my time, uneasy, my mind confused, too tired to think.

Something about this day brought back the memory of an evening in Sydney, during the World Congress of 1989, when alone in my room, getting ready for a gala event presented by Subud Austria I broke down. That congress was the first without Bapak, and the pressure on the IHs was tremendous. Beside the plenary sessions, the workshops, the endless daily meetings and the many issues that demanded immediate attention, there was also criticism, mud-slinging, power play and back stabbing (as Lorraine loved to say: we were the ducks in the shooting

148

gallery), and I, barely recognizing myself, kept acting and talking and caring and smiling and going on and on, like a dancing puppet on strings... So I prayed 'please God, let me be, give me some rest.'

Thus, as I joined the crowd to watch the procession of 'Debutantes' waltzing away with their escorts to the lilting music of Johan Strauss, I disintegrated. This 'Viennese Ball', which promised to be a pinnacle of entertainment, became for me on the one hand a shallow, irrelevant spectacle and, on the other, a disturbing reminder of bygone days that raised the spectre of unbearable thoughts. Thrust into such darkness, I rushed back to my room, sobbing uncontrollably, until a little mocking voice piped up: 'But you just said you wanted peace, so we let go of your strings...'

Now it seemed that the Grand Puppeteer had let go of my strings again... Moving restlessly about the house, it was some time before the noises from the outside registered; a kitten mewed under the open window; a neighbour was working with a power-tool; (who dares make noises at such a late hour?) a bird trilled. And suddenly, alert, I thought; 'Wait a minute, it's after midnight! Since when do birds sing in the middle of the night? There are no nightingales in this part of the world!' The cat mewed again, the wheezy power tool resumed its racket, the bird trilled; and then it clicked – it was a bird that was making all these sounds!

The Audubon Field Guide identified it as a Gray Catbird, a Mockingbird variety. The bird repeated its sequence of mewing, wheezing, and trilling many more times, adding other songs to its repertoire, so that at one point it seemed as if the hedge was full of song birds – truly a virtuoso performance, a kind of one-bird opera. The moon shone high in the sky, the tall cedars silhouetted against it, and the bird kept singing its heart out. It lasted well over an hour.

The catbird stayed in my garden for three days – a sleek gray bird with a long tail flitting back and forth among the shrubs; but it didn't sing again, and though the book informs me that it is a common visitor in suburban gardens, I haven't heard or seen it before or since.

As for me, there was nothing common about *this* bird. I believed then, and still do, that there was a purpose to its visit that night. Instinctively I guessed that it was a herald signalling a turning point in my life; that it predicted a change that concerned my creative work and my immediate future. I sensed that my life would become very solitary but also, that whatever would happen, I will not be alone – the bird was the sign; God was with me.

In August we took a three-week vacation in the Gaspé, Quebec. As we drove further and further away from Ontario, and as we spent our days in that foreign and beautiful land, I'd catch myself thinking: 'thank God I am away from Subud! I wish I could stay away for ever…I don't want to return; being a helper is a thankless job; I don't want to see or talk with anyone – I want to leave Subud!'

This was dreadful, almost suicidal; Subud was my life! But I was so burdened and tired; my chest felt tight and nothing felt right; all I wanted was to stop the world and get off. Accordingly, on the long drive back, the car, mirroring my state (though at the time I didn't make the connection), lost its power. The alternator wouldn't charge the battery; we couldn't drive without lights and had to spend another night on the road, until the 'tired' vehicle was repaired.

It would take much longer to 'repair' me…

The verdict via testing was that I should give up immediately my helper's duties and any other involvement in Subud; I needed a complete sabbatical. The local group, which had been doing latihan in our house for eight years, was given notice and they left by New Year's. Only then did I begin to breathe more freely; I never noticed the heaviness that lingered in the house after group latihans.

My sabbatical grew into a full-scale retirement. For over four years I stayed away from Subud members and close friends alike. I had become overly sensitive to people, absorbing their inner state, consequently becoming terribly burdened and continuously sick.

This was an unfamiliar and unsettling situation. I had heard of people who had left Subud after years of latihan and commitment, and I used to question their motives. Now I myself was experiencing great difficulties. But to leave Subud was not an option for me. And why would I want to leave the latihan in the first place (if one could ever really leave it) when it has given me such a profound sense of reality; when it is the deepest and truest way I know to communicate with the Almighty? And who said that the road would be easy?

I didn't leave Subud but did latihan alone. I learned to accept with equanimity the intense spiritual process I was going through. Often it was tormenting and painful, at times erratic and unpredictable; every day seemed to bring new questions and new struggles; but it was also an incredibly rich and fulfilling time. As the bird 'predicted' I discovered a new and meaningful direction in my work; I had many extraordinary dreams and received countless insights regarding my life and life in general. However, at one point, when my inner life became so disruptive that I wasn't sure I could cope, believing that I was on the verge of losing my sanity, I wrote to Ibu Rahayu; was I still on the right track? The following is an excerpt from her letter:

11 October 1995
'What you are experiencing now is the process of a crisis. Indeed crises take many forms. Actually you are a sensitive person. In the process of a crisis indeed there is a strong contact with God, so that it is as if you can fathom the feeling and the situation of other people. Actually this is only as a witness, that the Power of God is one.

'The steps that you have taken are right, to stop being a helper, and if necessary, do not follow the group latihan.

'What is best for the meantime, is if you latihan by yourself at home only twice a week, and not for too long a time. If you feel something, mention the name of God, and say within yourself, "God, I ask to be protected and all problems I return to the One Almighty God." This is training also, so that as time goes on you will become strong and normal when you face any situation.

'There is a time when we need to develop just for ourselves. When you have been in Subud a long time and you have many helpers' duties, possibly you now need to feel and deepen your own latihan.

'Live normally with your family and keep close to other Subud members.

'I pray that this process will end quickly, and that you will benefit more from the latihan kejiwaan of Subud in your life.'

If I Am Not For Myself, Who Then?

My crisis was in its third year and my inner life had become a series of continuous upheavals. To help me cope I began saying regular prayers. As I do not follow a religion, I composed my own, and every night before going to bed I prayed for protection and guidance, for the well being of my loved ones, for the growth of Subud, for harmony, and for world peace. There came a time when I didn't dare NOT to pray.

Then in the fall of 1997 I began to be frequented by a strange physical phenomenon; a recurring nightly seizure that was unlike anything I had ever experienced. Mostly it affected the inner right thigh and felt like an electrical current travelling from the brain. It was excruciatingly painful and very scary. The only way to ease it was to jump out of bed, put my full weight on the leg, pace the floor gritting my teeth, so as not to wake Edgar, and wait for it to subside.

I didn't want to consult a doctor or confide in the helpers – I was now on my own and had to face whatever it was alone. I assumed it was part of the crisis, that I was expected to learn from it and that it would end without medical intervention. Nevertheless each night I prayed fervently for help; I even invoked Bapak to intercede on my behalf, and, for good measure, kept his photo in the bedroom…all to no avail. The seizure could happen at any time, but mostly it attacked between 2:00 and 3:00am – the hour of despair. I slept lightly and nervously. I didn't record the frequency or duration of these episodes; they might have been few and far between, but I remember them as a time of terror that would never end.

And then one night, around 4:00 am, the hour of grace, while standing on the cold bathroom floor waiting for an oncoming assault, a thought pierced through the stupefying haze of fear and sleeplessness. 'There must be a way to cope! If I ask I'll be shown how!' And forcing myself not to give in to the mounting panic, I urgently tested: 'How should I be when the seizure begins?'

It all happened in a split second. I became vigilant and felt a sudden strength pulling me together, and then, unexpectedly, I spoke out loud the Hebrew words, '*Im ein ani li mi li?*' The first line of the famous saying by Rabi Hillel: 'If I am not for myself, who then? And if I am for myself, who am I? And if not now when?' Repeating the line over and over again, feeling the words imparting a formidable inner strength; directly the seizure that was as yet in its early stages, abated and disappeared – never to return.

This was a stunning lesson. I used to pay lip service to the saying that God helps those who help themselves. But being thus schooled by a heavy-handed 'tutor', the message was clear: for me the glorified shopping lists to God and the crying like a baby to a remote Deity are worthless; it is within me that His help is manifested. Doing the latihan, I should have known better!

And as it so often happens, while I was working on this story, aware that I am encroaching on a subject I am the least qualified to write about, I came across a quotation from Bapak about prayer.

> 'The fact is that whatever your prayer, whatever you ask God, God will always grant you, no matter what it is, provided you are in a state of peace, acceptance, submission and patience. In that state the thing you ask does not come from your own imagination. For as long as what you ask is still a construct of your own desires, it is impossible for God to give it to you. But once what you ask comes truly from your white blood and not from your red, whatever it is God will grant it. So if God never gives you what you ask, the fault again is your own." (83 CDK 2 Cilandak January 9 1983)

But the question of prayer was only one of the reasons for this experience; the other was far more urgent and important. For with this saying I was given a *tool* to gauge my awareness of the inner 'I'. At any time, during any activity, I would check; '*Im ein ani li mi li?*' In other words: am I connected to my inner guidance, or am I somewhere else flying kites? And instantly the words would snap me back and get me in focus.

Thus an old saying that as children we rattled down like a tongue twister – misleading in its terseness and playfulness – became a tangible tool, as practical as a road map or a compass.

And when, shortly after, my life's situation took a dramatic turn for the worse and for months I could not do the latihan (nor much else), it was this saying that helped navigate me back to my inner *self*, and the guidance and strength therein.

* * *

March 11, 1998. After breakfast I lingered over a cup of coffee, my mood serene, enjoying the bright spring-like morning. I was aware of a keen sense of anticipation, as if a major change awaited me around the corner. This is the Year of the Tiger, I thought – the year I turn sixty. I speculated that my Subud crisis would be over soon – I could sense it in my bones – which meant that I'd return to group latihans and 'normality'. I wondered what was next in store for me. Would I be permitted to exhibit my work? – Since testing had indicated repeatedly that I should not exhibit.

It had been four years since my last exhibition and the canvases were crowding the basement; I thought it was utterly senseless! Why was I forbidden anyway? Was it because of my over-sensitivity, my attitudes, or the nature of my work? Couldn't I just go ahead and exhibit without testing? It was after all an enterprise, a worldly matter that shouldn't be tested at all! (Yet in previous attempts I had received strong indications that I was going against what was right for me…)

Thus I kept on pushing and arguing with God, when suddenly I felt very queer and had to put my head on the table. Fearfully, I thought, 'okay God, I surrender, I'll stop this bickering' … but then I sensed that half of my face had gone numb…

I'll spare you the gory details. This was the onslaught of a full-blown stroke that landed me in hospital with my whole left side paralyzed – heavy and helpless like a beached whale. There was nothing further 'spiritual' about the whole mess, only that it heralded the end of the crisis.

Reconciliation

A t the back of a sketchbook from 1996, I found the following entry. 'Today is the 29th anniversary of my mother's death. Yesterday while walking about in the Etobicoke neighbourhood, I saw a woman with short white hair and energetic movements getting out of her car and going up a driveway; she reminded me of my mother, and filled with longing I thought, "Would that my mother came thus to visit me!"

'I must say that this is a first; to be longing for her, for the way she used to be… Yet a faint distant memory comes back, of sitting together over a cup of coffee and having a good conversation…We had had some good moments too.

'This was a Gift! It was as if, in that split second of longing, a locked door opened a fraction, to let me witness a sliver of love – like a miracle. And I stood on the sidewalk filled with wonderment; such an intense moment, and yet such a nothing. Here I was in this unfamiliar neighbourhood, waiting for Ilana to finish her music lesson, idly inspecting gardens…. I put the full meaning out of my mind. Yes, it was extraordinary, but this was not the place, nor the time to be overwhelmed.'

But slowly things began to work themselves to the surface. For earlier that year I had done a series of drawings that dealt with the question of who am I or, more specifically, what were the 'gifts' I inherited from my parents and grandparents? I had already done a couple of paintings on the subject, but it was only a year later that I dared tackle the drawing for My Mother's Gift and flesh it out into a painting. The drawing represents a schematic sideways image of my mother's watchful face, which dominates the left side of the page; above it is a grieving figure

156

with a wedge pointing to its chest; and from its hand, in the centre of the page, a spiral cascades towards a crouching figure at the bottom.

Working on the painting was a double challenge. Emotionally it was like attempting the Everest; and artistically it was tricky and elusive. I worked on it on and off for many months. The process was slow and difficult. Often I could feel my mother's presence and 'hear' her sharp, chiding voice, so that filled with the same old anger I would have to stop the work. And yet I didn't dare to test the subject; it was too volatile, and I wasn't ready. But in the end it had to be done.

Bapak would ask members sometimes to receive how their inner state had been when they were young, say at the age of ten or fifteen, which gave me the idea to explore my attitudes towards my mother at various stages of my life, going all the way back to infancy.

To receive my inner state as a newborn felt surprisingly normal and familiar, and yet the outcome of this test changed in one fell swoop everything I had known about my life. For my receiving indicated that from the very beginning it was I who didn't love and accept my mother – that I had invested all my baby love in my father. How ironic! Nowadays much is made of bonding, that magical tie between mother and child that should be formed within the first hours of birth. Yet my receiving implied otherwise, as if I, the newborn had already made the choice. Or was there no choice and everything had been decreed?

So how does a mother feel when her baby rejects her? And how does she feel when she cannot love her baby? It was only fair that I reversed the questions and tested for my mother too. To receive her point of view was devastating. She did so try; she did her best to love me but her efforts were contrived and she was perplexed and distraught, and the older I got the more unhappy she became. I also received that it directly affected her health, her ulcer and high blood pressure, and may even have brought on the fatal heart attack.

The enormity of this secret was overwhelming. I stood there, in our basement-cum-latihan room, suspended in time, crushed by the knowledge of the terrible sins I had committed against my mother and stunned by the inevitability of it all! The perpetual self-image of the wronged child dissolved into a deep shame. I wasn't the only victim in this relationship. And the only thing I could think of was how my poor mother had suffered and how she was not to blame.

Was there a light at the end of the tunnel? There was nothing I could do but surrender. The ensuing latihan was a tormented and anguished prayer for forgiveness. When nothing was left but exhaustion and emptiness, a miraculous feeling of lightness engulfed me, like a river of compassion, gently pulling me in, washing away the darkness and restoring the calm.

The painting in its final transformation acquired vivid colours, a dramatic division of light and dark, and an allusion to the stage, all superimposed onto the original introverted drawing. It had evolved into a testimonial, a kind of formal memento to peacemaking. Accordingly I changed its title to 'Reconciliation'. Two years later, on an impulse, I submitted it to the local annual art show and it was accepted.

We didn't go to the formal opening, but intended to visit the gallery at the Mayor's levee on New Year's Day. Outside, in front of the Mississauga Civic Centre, people skated on an ice rink. Inside, in the marbled foyer, I met old acquaintances, drank hot chocolate, listened to the children's orchestra, shook hands with our intrepid mayor, the Hon. Mrs. Hazel McCallion, and only then went to check out the art gallery in the east wing.

'Reconciliation' was the first painting to meet the eye upon entering the main gallery. It hung on a prominent wall all by itself, the spotlights giving it extra drama – and it looked fabulous!

A month later, photographs of the award ceremony (to which I didn't go) appeared in the local newspaper. My painting didn't win a prize, but the awards were presented in front of it. I now have photographs of unknown people shaking hands with unknown officials, all smiling broadly – in front of the 'Reconciliation'. There must be a meaning to all this!

Beit-Yitzhak Revisited

Yesterday I phoned my sister-in-law, Hanna, in Israel, to congratulate her on her 80th birthday. She was surprised and pleased. If Stephan had been alive they would have celebrated their birthday together, she said; it was a pity. We had a long conversation.

Beit-Yitzhak today is a close-knit and vibrant community. Most of the people I grew up with had remained in the village, surrounded by their children and grandchildren.

Everyone, of course, knows everybody else, and Hanna gave me all the information I wanted and more. It is astonishing that people still ask after me, as they did whenever I'd arrive for a visit. Older members would then stop me on the street; 'You must be *Magdalenchen ja*? I still remember you when you were *Ein kleines blondes Madchen mit Rattenschwenzchen*' (a little blond girl with braids).

Even so something about that place had been pushing me away. I have been in Canada for thirty years and have never returned for a visit; I don't believe I ever will.

It was the eve of Rosh Hashanah; I had come to Beit-Yitzhak for Hanna's traditional family get-together. I had evaded it for two years, but had run out of excuses. In the meantime I had joined Subud, had seen Bapak in Germany, had been appointed as helper and had done my first Ramadan fast. My life had become a succession of remarkable inner and outer changes, like rafting on a fast flowing river with an ever-changing landscape. Yet at my brother's home everything was as it had always been. Hanna, fussing over the meal in the kitchen, greeted me with a flustered look; Stephan was somewhere out on the farm; my nine-year-old nephew was as spoiled as ever (he turned out very well indeed), and my two nieces were growing into beautiful, self-absorbed teenagers.

I went to visit a neighbour, Mrs. Spier – a lovely old lady. She and her late husband had been close friends of my parents. I took a walk to admire Stephan's pecan grove and cactus garden. I didn't visit anyone else; I never did.

Helping Hanna in the kitchen I became aware of an unfamiliar surge of love towards her – a peculiar sensation. We had always had a strained relationship, tiptoeing guardedly around each other. No doubt this was the working of the latihan. Hanna too noticed something different about me and remarked how I had changed – for the better – asking about Subud with genuine interest.

But shortly after dinner I became unwell with sharp pains in my midriff. It wasn't because of something I had eaten. I thought it was the kind of pain my mother would get sometimes, and that my present 'openness' had invited a host of negative associations connected to this place, that were crowding my inner and bloating me to an intolerable point of pain. After all, Stephan's home, though renovated and enlarged, was my childhood home. I even slept in what used to be my old bedroom. My father had died in the adjacent room.

The pain persisted through the night. I knew a latihan would help but there was no place to do it and besides, I was already too ill.

In the morning I insisted on returning to Jerusalem. No, I didn't need a doctor. No, I couldn't wait till the holiday was over. Hanna was concerned and perplexed, but I couldn't explain.

Stephan drove me in his jeep to the main intersection, where I waited for a taxi service, *Sherut*, to take me to Tel Aviv and from there to Jerusalem. There is no public transport on high holidays, and there was little else; the highway was virtually deserted. Eventually a lone Sherut did materialize. The ride was long and painful and, to my embarrassment, I was repeatedly sick in the car.

Upon arriving home I phoned my helper, Miriam Karin. She came and took me over to her place. And since I was in no condition to do latihan by myself, she did it for me; that is to say, she did a 'latihan for the sick'. Lying on her bed, faintly conscious of her starting the latihan, I immediately fell asleep. I awoke to see Miriam sitting peacefully in her armchair doing embroidery. The pain was completely gone. I felt wonderfully released, though fragile, as if an old skin – like the dead skin of a snake – had been peeled off, to leave me exposed like a newborn.

Neither Miriam nor I were able to understand what it was all about, but a long time went by before I dared visit Beit-Yitzhak again. On that occasion nothing remarkable happened; however I remained extra vigilant.

I received the answer in a recent latihan – some 37 years after the event. It was a stunning revelation, yet so logical; why didn't I ever think about it? The relentless force that was pushing me away from Beit-Yitzhak had originated with my mother! I received how hopeless her situation was and how imprisoned and trapped she felt living there. The fact that she never voiced it was because it was buried deep in her unconscious. It was left to me, by having adopted and internalizing her attitude – which I had been acting upon blindly all my life – to fulfil her destiny.

Adama

It is an extra bonus to receive in latihan songs from one's childhood and youth. They are an unparalleled elixir of life or, in plainer words, a first rate pick-me-up. For I don't believe that there's anything that can come even close to the optimism of a ten-year-old, or the life-energy of a teenager! And this is what these songs in the latihan impart to one's tired spirit and aging body.

Recently, in a latihan, such a long forgotten song resurfaced. Its name is *Adama*, which means earth, and its words, roughly translated, are as follows.

'Adama, adama,
In the plain and the height,
In rain and shine,
You are our mother,
The mother of man and all living.'

Naturally it was a very solemn, patriotic song – all the better to poke fun at. Thus we would roar it on the bus, on our way to school, to irritate the suffering driver and the indignant   passengers.

And here I was singing it in latihan and laughing like a carefree, saucy kid. And I had to own that Beit-Yitzhak wasn't such a bad place in which to grow up after all, even though deep down my unhappiness was mounting. There are many memories, average childhood memories, neither good nor bad, that have also an undeniable place in the bedrock of my persona.

The group of children I grew up with was singular in that it was the first, large, same age group in the village (about 13 kids to begin with, which slowly grew as newcomers arrived). Hence from kindergarten onwards, for better or for worse, whether one liked it or didn't, we acted always as a group, in school, in town, or on the beach – we were the

'Beit-Yitzhakers'. This interdependence and togetherness infuriated and frustrated me beyond measure; one simply couldn't escape it.

Even so I cannot deny that we had some good times. There were night games and day games; soccer, ping-pong, and ball games; mock gang-fights and pranks; stealing and vandalizing. In the summer on Saturdays we'd hang out on the beach and go to the movies in the evening. In the spring we'd take bicycle outings or hiking trips. There were awkward parties and dances, bonfires and folk dancing.

And I never missed a thing.

I have destroyed most of my photographs of that time and these memories have become a closed book. But I did retain some gentler images that – like an improbable whiff from the ocean that is carried on the wind across half a continent – are evocative of the place and my childhood, which I present here with a cautious nostalgia…

Did you know that when you hang upside-down from the railing at the community centre you can see far beyond the village, past the swampy field where the narcissus grow, as far as the town of Avichail? This upside-down world is always beautiful – always untarnished.

A gigantic yellow moon is rising over the darkening fields. I stand on the porch beside my mother, watching silently. It is a ritual. My mother takes my hand and we begin to sing softly in German, *Der Mond ist aufgegangen.* It is an old German song and it gives me the shivers without fail.

> 'The moon is rising,
> Golden stars sparkle
> In the sky so clear and bright,
> The wood is dark and silent,
> And from the meadows rises,
> The mist so white and wonderful.'

The first autumn rains have packed down the sands. Now we meet towards dusk for circle dancing. We sing and clap while a lone child skips in the middle choosing a partner.

'I stand in the circle and look around,
I offer my hand to a friend,
In the forest – in the forest we'll dance.'

I sing with pleasure but my heart is timid; will somebody dance with me?

'We'll build a bridge together
Over the raging river.'

The construction of the new silo in the centre across from our house is slowly approaching its completion. We have been playing on the site for months. Now the latest thrill is to jump from the flat roof onto a mountain of hay. I dare not – I am afraid of heights. But my friends egg me on: 'It's fun, Jump!'

One Friday afternoon, the workers gone home early, alone on the site, I muster my courage and jump. It feels wonderful! I have done it! So I climb back and jump once more – only this time I sprain my ankle and have to stay in bed for days.

It is early summer on a quiet Shabbat morning. The air is fresh with the smell of dew and freshly cut grass. I am in the back of the house in the shade, practicing assiduously the handstand against the wall.

It is a week after my father's death and a new girl has come to the village. Her name is Nurit. Overcoming my shyness, I walk resolutely down the street towards her house. I know I am the first to visit her and I know that she will be my best friend.

Nurit is a dark, handsome girl, a tomboy, an athlete, and a lover of animals; she is funny, unaffected, and she has become my best friend.

We take summer jobs together working in the fields; long hot days of backbreaking work and a great time to fool around.

One humid hot evening, sitting on our porch, Nurit says wistfully, 'I am dying for a slice of watermelon, do you think Tzvi has any ripe ones?' (His field touches our property.)

'Let's go and look.'

We sneak into the field under the cover of darkness – the watermelons appear like large black blobs and our bare feet get tangled in the vine. Nurit whispers, 'how can you tell a ripe one if you can't see the colour?'

'You tap on it, it should sound hollow,'

'They all sound the same to me,'

'Then we should cut out a small triangle and taste – that's how the watermelon vendors do it.'

Nurit gets up promptly, heading towards the house. 'I'll fetch a knife.'

'No! Wait, I was joking, Tzvi will kill us!'

'He won't mind a few watermelons.'

She returns with a knife and giggling madly we cut triangles into many watermelons until a worthy one is found.

When next time we report for work I suspect, by the twinkle in his eyes, that Tzvi knows who the vandals are, but he doesn't say a word. We continue to work in his fields all that summer – though repentant: Tzvi didn't deserve our shabby trick.

On the edge of the Hanes property towering over the road stands a majestic cypress tree. Every time I pass it I look up into its tightly shaped boughs. It is a tree in prayer and I know that I am on holy ground. The feeling of holiness is palpable and constant; it is always present. I stand beneath it transported, aware of an existence without questions, of oneness with the tree, with the deep sky above it, with the moon, and with myself. It is a perfect moment – a perfect Yes.

BEYOND THE BREAKERS

GLOSSARY

Bapak – An Indonesian word meaning father or respected older man. In Subud, the founder of Subud is referred to as Pak Subuh or Bapak. His full name is Muhammad Subuh Sumohadiwidjojo.

Crisis – The term crisis, as used in Subud, is a state of instability caused by a person experiencing deep spiritual changes. Some crises are brought about by an overly strong desire to speed up the process of the latihan; others are received as a gift when the person is ready.

Dewan – An Indonesian word for council, board or team.

Helpers – In Subud, a 'helper' is a person who fills a certain support role, which includes giving explanations about Subud, arranging openings, scheduling group latihans and supporting the members through the process of their spiritual training. Helpers assist at local, regional, national, and international levels.

Ibu – Indonesian word meaning Mrs or mother; in Subud, if used alone, it refers to Bapak's second wife, Siti Sumari.

Ibu Rahayu – Bapak's eldest daughter: Ibu Siti Rahayu Wiryohudoyo.

Kejiwaan – an Indonesian word meaning spiritual or pertaining to the soul.

Latihan – 'The reappearance of a primordial Power hidden within human beings and all creatures. This Power manifests itself in spontaneous bodily movements and utterances, a mood of tranquillity and joy, clarity of awareness, and love for the Divine. It works progressively to cleanse and harmonize the conflicting elements of our being, to heal and to illuminate. The latihan cannot be learned, but it can be transmitted from one person to another.' – Leonard Priestley

Opening – one's first latihan, or spiritual training exercise, is called the opening.

Pendopo – Indonesian; a porch or veranda; also an auditorium.

Prihatin – An Indonesian word, prihatin means asceticism. Individual Subud members sometimes voluntarily engage in fasting on Mondays and Thursdays or in other ways of reducing pleasure, in the hope of improving their life situation.

Ramadan – Annual Muslim fast; some Subud members observe the fast of Ramadan to increase their spiritual awareness.

Selamatan – An Indonesian word, selamat, means safe, good, congratulations, good luck. A selamatan is an occasion of well-wishing, a Javanese ceremonial meal to mark or celebrate an occasion, such as a wedding, a move to a new home, a promotion, the recovery of a family member from illness or the passing of a relative or friend.

Shiv'a – In Judaism, a seven-day period of mourning

Subud – An acronym formed from three Javanese words (originally Sanskrit): Susila, Budhi and Dharma. Susila means living in accordance with the highest moral principles; Budhi is the Power of awakening that is within each person; and Dharma is submission to the divine Source of one's being. Although spiritual in content, Subud does not constitute a religion. It includes members of every religion, as well as many people who are not adherents of any religion.

Should you wish to find out more about Subud, here are two suggestions:

- A Subud group may be listed in your telephone directory. If not,
- Visit www.subud.com on the Internet. Click on the "Subud Contacts" link. Scroll down the list of countries, click on your country and contact information will appear. There are Subud groups in over seventy countries.

Testing – In the event of a serious spiritual problem, it is possible to seek guidance or clarification directly through the latihan by a procedure called 'testing'. This is simply to receive the latihan in response to a particular question.

Shabbat – Hebrew, the Sabbath, the Jewish day of rest.

Subud Organization – The Subud organisation exists to connect individuals practising the Subud spiritual training. The association of Subud is democratically organised. The World Subud Council, consisting of representatives from all the nations in Subud and its executive body, the International Subud Committee, carry out the aims of Subud, looking after the needs of the members and setting up general welfare projects through a division called Susila Dharma. Every four years there is a world congress held in a different country.

Tanach – The Hebrew Bible. Tanach is a Hebrew acronym, formed from the initial Hebrew letters of Torah (Pentateuch), Nevi'im (Prophets) and Ketuvim (Writings)

Wadi – Arabic word for a dry riverbed.

Wisma Subud – Subud community in Cilandak, Jakarta.

5716263R0

Made in the USA
Lexington, KY
10 June 2010